More praise for *The Reciprocity Advantage*

"This is a thinker's book that will make companies and leaders face the future with potential answers rather than uncertainty. A practical read from start to finish."
—Nigel Travis, Chairman and CEO, Dunkin' Brands

"If your business is squeezed by ever-tightening margins and confronted daily by disruptive forces, understanding your reciprocity advantage will open you to the potential of nontraditional partnerships as a path to large-scale growth."
—Donald Hall, Jr., CEO, Hallmark

"Few industries have been more disrupted by the Internet than news media and print publishing. This new 'how to' guide provides a road map that can allow publishing companies to become disruptors and create a bright future for themselves and the people they serve."
—Bill Toler, CEO, Swift Communications

"In *The Reciprocity Advantage*, Ronn and Johansen provide a new golden rule for business: give to grow and share to scale. A must-read."
—Scott Anthony, Managing Partner, Innosight, and author of *The First Mile* and *The Little Black Book of Innovation*

"Every winning strategy is based on a compelling insight, and *The Reciprocity Advantage* is loaded with insight. Capturing a reciprocity advantage will be the next strategic advantage."
—William G. Pietersen, Professor of the Practice of Management, Columbia Business School, and author of *Strategic Learning*

"Bob Johansen and Karl Ronn have produced a book that offers masterful insight into one of the defining features of today's world: advantage through reciprocal value creation. Our old win-lose models are no longer fit for purpose. The best businesses today are aiming higher. Bob and Karl's vision will help any leader unlock new forms of value with new thinking."
—Aron Cramer, President and CEO, Business for Social Responsibility

"*The Reciprocity Advantage* is required reading for my Marketing for Social Profit students. It gives readers at all levels of business experience perspectives and actionable information to enhance business and innovation results. Anyone interested in growing and making a positive collaborative impact should read this book."
—Linda L. Golden, Marlene and Morton Meyerson Centennial Professor in Business, The University of Texas at Austin

"With their uncanny knack for seeing the future, Bob Johansen and Karl Ronn offer a priceless gift—a fresh, practical strategy for collaboration that can advance both margin and mission in organizations of all kinds. Leaders at every level will benefit from their wisdom."
—John R. Ryan, President and CEO, Center for Creative Leadership

THE
RECIPROCITY
ADVANTAGE

Other Books by Bob Johansen

Get There Early

Leaders Make the Future

Upsizing the Individual in the Downsized Organization
(with Rob Swigart)

Global Work
(with Mary O'Hara-Devereaux)

Leading Business Teams

Groupware

Teleconferencing and Beyond

Electronic Meetings
(with Jacques Vallee and Kathleen Spangler)

THE RECIPROCITY ADVANTAGE

A NEW WAY TO PARTNER FOR INNOVATION AND GROWTH

BOB JOHANSEN and KARL RONN

BK

Berrett–Koehler Publishers, Inc.
San Francisco
a BK Business book

Berrett-Koehler Publishers, Inc.
235 Montgomery Street, Suite 650
San Francisco, CA 94104-2916
Tel: (415) 288-0260   Fax: (415) 362-2512
www.bkconnection.com

Ordering Information
Quantity sales. Special discounts are available on quantity purchases by corporations, associations, and others. For details, contact the "Special Sales Department" at the Berrett-Koehler address above.
Individual sales. Berrett-Koehler publications are available through most book stores. They can also be ordered directly from Berrett-Koehler: Tel: (800) 929-2929; Fax: (802) 864-7626; www.bkconnection.com.
Orders for college textbook/course adoption use. Please contact Berrett-Koehler: Tel: (800) 929-2929; Fax: (802) 864-7626.
Orders by U.S. trade bookstores and wholesalers. Please contact Ingram Publisher Services: Tel: (800) 509-4887; Fax: (800) 838-1149; E-mail: customer.service@ ingrampublisherservices.com; or visit www.ingrampublisherservices.com/Ordering for details about electronic ordering.

Berrett-Koehler and the BK logo are registered trademarks of Berrett-Koehler Publishers, Inc.

Printed in the United States of America

Berrett-Koehler books are printed on long-lasting acid-free paper. When it is available, we choose paper that has been manufactured by environmentally responsible processes. These may include using trees grown in sustainable forests, incorporating recycled paper, minimizing chlorine in bleaching, or recycling the energy produced at the paper mill.

CATALOGING-IN-PUBLICATION DATA
Johansen, Robert
The reciprocity advantage : a new way to partner for innovation & growth / Bob Johansen, Karl Ronn.
    pages   cm. — (A BK business book)
SUMMARY: "Bestselling author and renowned futurist Bob Johansen combines with business innovation guru Karl Ronn to produce a visionary book on the biggest innovation opportunity in history: giving away what you have to learn how to make money in new ways. They call it the reciprocity advantage" —Provided by publisher.
    Includes bibliographical references and index.
    ISBN 978-1-62656-106-9 (hardback)
    1. Reciprocity (Psychology)—Social aspects.   2. Social interaction.
3. Cooperation.   4. Competition.   5. Success in business.   I. Ronn, Karl.   II. Title.
    HM1111.J64 2014
    302'.14—dc23   2014019674

19   18   17   16   15   14   10   9   8   7   6   5   4   3   2   1

Project Management and book design: BookMatters; copyediting: Tanya Grove; indexing: Leonard Rosenbaum. Cover design: Archie Ferguson.

To Robin & Elizabeth,
Our life partners

CONTENTS

PREFACE

Reciprocity and advantage—long thought of separately—will become increasingly synergistic. The next competitive advantage will be *reciprocity* advantage. This book shows you how to create a reciprocity advantage for your business.

The disruptions of the next decade will require organizations to think about and practice reciprocity on a massive scale. Now is the time to move, to ride the coming disruptions to your own benefit—and to the benefit of others.

Reciprocity will be key to business growth in the future. If you can create a reciprocity advantage, you will be able to grow your business in new ways. You may not have to do so right now, but you will within a decade. This is a future you cannot avoid.

Reciprocity is a means for disruptive business innovation and growth. Developing a reciprocity advantage will require intelligent giving that will lead to discoveries of how to make money in new ways. Think: give to grow.

The concept of reciprocity is rising and is going to work in new ways. It makes good business sense and is a better way to live. Having a reciprocity advantage will be essential to thrive in the coming world.

The goal of this book is to seed a transformational yet practical conversation about both reciprocity and advantage—simultaneously and from two very different perspectives. Bob Johansen is a practicing

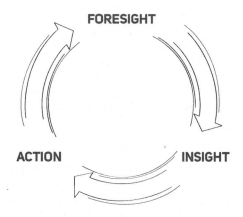

Figure 1: Foresight Insight Action
(Source: IFTF).

futurist, while Karl Ronn is a product innovation practitioner. Mapping the territory of reciprocity advantage requires both visionary foresight and practical innovation, combined in new ways.

Bob has more than 30 years' experience at Institute for the Future (IFTF) in Silicon Valley as a ten-year forecaster, with remarkable accuracy. Bob helps top leaders and rising stars draw insight from external foresight.

With more than 25 years of experience with a wide range of companies, Karl is an expert on disruptive innovation, which lies between insight and action. Karl was a key innovator behind new billion-dollar businesses like Swiffer, Febreze, and Mr. Clean Magic Eraser, for example.

Procter & Gamble has long been a supporter of IFTF. Karl met Bob when Karl was at P&G, and they have known each other for many years. Karl was one of those IFTF clients who managed to translate foresight into insight and action in order to grow P&G's business. After Karl left P&G to start his own businesses and advise others, he got the chance to work with Bob on innovation strategies that take into account the external future forces of the next decade.

Together, Bob and Karl have created a formula that looks ahead ten years but also outlines an action plan for the next 90 days so that you can begin to create your own reciprocity advantage right away. The model introduced here not only helps corporations discover their own reciprocity advantages, it can also be applied to individuals.

We look to the future, but this is a future that leaders can begin making today. We invite you into this conversation.

Bob Johansen & Karl Ronn
Palo Alto, 2014

The New Way
to Grow a Business

Reciprocity and *advantage* are two words that are rarely used together. Advantage is basic to business. Reciprocity is basic to life.

In the present, most people think of reciprocity *or* advantage. In the future, this magical juxtaposition—reciprocity *and* advantage—will spark new business models for innovation and growth.

Reciprocity is the practice of exchanging with others for mutual benefit. Reciprocity is a very old idea in a very new context: the shift from today's Internet to tomorrow's cloud-served supercomputing ecosystem. The cloud will make it possible to create more businesses with more partners globally connected. The cloud will become the world's biggest amplifier, as we discuss in Chapter 8. The currency of the cloud will be reciprocity.

Reciprocity lives in the space between transactions (buying and selling) and philanthropy (giving for good causes).

Advantage lives in a world where businesses seek a superior position that leads to profit and growth. Advantage means achieving a winning position, but it doesn't necessarily mean that others must lose in order for you to win.

Reciprocity advantage will be a new type of competitive advantage.

- It will be grounded in a right-of-way that you already own.

- It will require that you give away some of your assets in

intelligent ways now in order to make money and grow your business over time. (Think: give to grow.)

- It can happen only when a company is able to *both* practice reciprocity *and* make money. (Reciprocity is the action; advantage is a gain that is earned by the action.)

- It must be designed to be massively scalable. Certainly, reciprocity can be practiced on a small scale, but this book focuses on creating large-scale growth through reciprocity.

This is a book that shows "what's next?" and shares what we believe will become the biggest innovation opportunity in history. Society is just entering a unique period when doing good and doing well will have to be combined in ways that have never before been imagined.

To ground the concept of reciprocity advantage in a current example, consider the evolution of TED over the last 30 years. Karl has participated in many TED conferences over the years and has followed its progress up close.

The visionary architect Richard Wurman foresaw the convergence of Technology, Entertainment, and Design (TED) and created a forum for innovators in these fields to discuss what he called "ideas worth spreading." He launched the first TED conference in 1984, before the virtual world we know today existed, back when Tim Berners-Lee was still writing a research proposal for what would become the World Wide Web, and almost ten years before we had browsers.

Wurman's vision was to create the world's most elite conference. The original TED conferences were expensive invitation-only events that took place in Monterey, California—a comfortable middle ground between Silicon Valley and Hollywood. A TED conference ticket was a hot commodity.

In 2001 Wurman sold TED to Chris Anderson's Sapling Foundation. Anderson pledged to keep the spirit of TED alive, but the great expansion of the Internet called for a new business model. The organizers realized that producing a great conference was no longer enough—people wanted to co-create with TED, not just sit back and listen. These "TED Talks" became available free to anyone in the world. By embracing social and technological change, TED prototyped its way into the future.

TEDx is the grassroots version of TED that has caught on around the world. Wherever people have "ideas worth spreading," a TEDx conference is likely to pop up. When the Sapling Foundation allowed anyone to run a TEDx conference, it created a huge new reciprocity advantage that builds on its past success. TED moved from a highly exclusive model to a radically democratic one. Meanwhile, the conference in its original format has continued to grow dramatically. By becoming more open and giving away assets associated with the TED brand, TED has become even more elite.

TEDx is a real-world example of reciprocity advantage. Value is exchanged for mutual benefit over time. The Sapling Foundation recognized that it owned assets it could share, and it partnered with others to augment its current business in a way that it could not do alone. TEDx has created new growth and also strengthened the core business. Others try to compete, but TED clearly has the advantage of increased global brand power, and it was accomplished by giving up control in ways that many traditional businesses would find unimaginable.

TEDx is not without its critics. In April 2013 the *Harvard Business Review*[1] published an article pointing out the impacts that poorly researched TEDx talks could have on the TED brand. Certainly the move to TEDx was risky and TED must be vigilant in how they manage all facets of their brand. However, the world has changed, and TEDx leverages those changes. TEDx is clearly differentiated from TED. TEDx is experimental and grassroots. TED is elite and controlled.

TEDx is a curated business, but it is not controlled. TED embraced the energy of the global community, and the result is that TEDx conferences have been held in more than 130 countries. TED provides advice to organizers of TEDx ahead of time, but TEDx events are done independently by the local organizers. The parent TED organization monitors outcomes and can promote good talks or effectively demote poor talks by not giving them a broader audience. TED and

TEDx coexist, but they are very different. By giving up control in TEDx, the TED brand gains new power through the grassroots reach. In fact, giving up control is *necessary* to gain this added power.

The *Harvard Business Review* article is aptly titled "When TED Lost Control of Its Crowd," but it misses the point—losing control is exactly what TED *must* do. Giving up control is often required in order to make money in new ways and start new businesses—to innovate in this emerging world. Curating is possible, but control is not. Lack of control certainly has risks (there will be bad TEDx talks), but the benefits far outweigh the risks. TED gave up considerable control, which has resulted in some criticism of quality, but the overall impact has been gigantic.

Here is Chris Anderson's own explanation of how TEDx works:[2]

> TED staff do not co-organise. We don't pre-screen speakers. That would defeat the purpose. This is a ground-up effort. It's only by genuinely granting power to local organizers that TEDx could have achieved its current scale. We have been astonished how good most of these events are. . . .
>
> Like Wikipedia, it shouldn't work but it does. And also like Wikipedia, occasionally mistakes creep in. Out of the 40,000 TEDx talk videos now online, about a dozen have been truly embarrassing, featuring pseudoscience or other absurdities.
>
> But the system self-corrects over time. Organisers learn from each other, and we are committed to empowering them with tools and advice that will allow each year's events to be a little better than the year before.

TED under Chris Anderson is focused on experimenting to learn, with as little direction as possible up front. Because TEDx experiments are everywhere, TED is a new model of inclusivity—even though the TED conference itself is still very exclusive. In this way, TED itself is both remarkably open *and* remarkably elite.

There will still be work ahead to ensure clarity on the differences between the TED brand and the sub-brand of TEDx. But this work will be agile curating—not traditional control of brands.

The journey came full circle in 2013 in Long Beach, where many of the TED Talks featured people who were identified via TEDx.

Brilliant innovation can come from anywhere, and now TED has the network to find it.

TED'S RECIPROCITY ADVANTAGE IN SUMMARY

What right-of-way does TED share with TEDx organizers? The TED organization has packaged its right-of-way as "TEDx-in-a-Box" and it includes

- the TED brand;
- the TED stage set and logo;
- the TED eighteen-minute high-production-values talk format.

Who are TED's partners? Passionate "TEDsters" around the world.

How did TED experiment to learn? TEDx began as an experiment in 2007. They used rapid prototypes to perfect their recipe for what to give away, what to control, and what to curate.

What assets does TED give away in order to learn?

- TED Talks from main TED event posted on the TED.com website.
- Recipes for organizing TEDx conferences.

How did TED scale? Volunteers organize TEDx events locally. Of course, not every TEDx is a success, so TED curates the results. Organizers of a good conference can give another TEDx; poor conferences aren't repeated. Only the very best talks are distributed through the cloud, growing their brand globally.

What is TED's reciprocity advantage? TEDx—the local version of TED staged anywhere—which complements and provides huge growth to the core TED brand and ideas worth spreading.

So What?
In five years TEDx has grown its grassroots effort to change the world with 30,000 "ideas worth spreading" presented in 133 countries. Just about every day, a TEDx event happens somewhere in the world.

Along the way, TEDx has also solved a problem for the main conference in today's world of instant news. In 2013, Chris Anderson used

TEDx and the local organizations as a talent search to find the very best people to bring to the main stage at the annual conference. This is an example of an advantage that TED gained from its reciprocity in allowing TEDx conferences to occur.

We find TED and TEDx fascinating, since they created a global brand based on reciprocity. As the World Wide Web took shape, TED embraced the turbulence and transformed itself from a company that put on elite conferences into a kind of organization that had never existed before. TEDx is a prototype for new business reciprocity-advantage models yet to be created. TED is just one example—there are many more.

The Basics of Reciprocity Advantage

Consider these basic definitions as we open the black box of reciprocity advantage.

> **trans·ac·tion** *(noun)* tran-ˈzak-shən: the instance of buying or selling something

Transactions are at the core of business today. In traditional business transactions, money is given for products received. You give me money; I give you goods in return. If you like the goods, you come back and give me more money for more goods. Both the buyer and the seller must see more value in giving up what they have (money or product).

Future forces will disrupt traditional transactional models, and margins will shrink. Transactions will continue to exist but will become increasingly commoditized. It will be increasingly difficult to run profitable businesses on this model alone. However, a transactional product may very well open the door to businesses with higher margins and higher values.

At the other extreme, consider

> **phi·lan·thro·py** *(noun)* fə-ˈlan(t)-thrə-pē: the desire to promote the welfare of others, expressed especially by generous donations to good causes

Philanthropy is motivated by altruism and the basic human instinct to give to others.

While business is stuck in the old world of transactions, philanthropy is stuck in the old world of grant giving—and often the accompanying burdensome bureaucracies. The big challenge for philanthropy is scaling: how to maximize the impact of good ideas that work locally. The same forces that are going to disrupt traditional transactional models will also disrupt philanthropy, albeit from different angles.

Philanthropy can be wonderful, but philanthropy is not what this book is about.

Reciprocity differs from transactions and philanthropy but has elements of both.

rec·i·proc·i·ty *(noun)* re-sə-ˈprä-s(ə-)tē: the practice of exchanging with others for mutual benefit

In a reciprocity-based business model, I give you something, and at some later point in time, I trust that I will learn how to get even more value back in return. While transactions are the currency of today's Internet, reciprocity will be the currency in tomorrow's world of cloud-served supercomputing. The cloud will allow individual companies to look out for the interests of their partners—and themselves—on an unprecedented scale.

A reciprocity advantage begins with smart giving, which is distinctly different from philanthropy or altruism. The reason for giving assets away isn't just about doing good—it's an important part of an ongoing value exchange spread over time where partners commit to looking out for each other as part of a shared vision.

Reciprocity advantage will live in the space between transactions and philanthropy—between list price and free. Businesses will be able to create new growth that would not have been possible to do on their own. And they will share some of that new value with others.

Harvard professor and expert on competitive strategy Michael Porter has studied this concept of "shared value."[3] His notion is that societal costs and benefits ought to be more integrated with businesses. He sees greater need for collaboration across these diverse organizations to identify societal needs and respond to them. Indeed, those who are closest to the problems are the best people to address them. In many cases, those are smaller businesses, governments, nonprofits, foundations, and even end users themselves. Large businesses have valuable assets, infrastructure, and know-how that make it easier and more efficient to scale solutions to these societal issues. In this way, business/community partnerships can spur innovation and growth that are profitable to the business and also benefit the community. Companies who find their own reciprocity advantage will be better partners in shared value initiatives.

We know from our discussions with others, however, that *reciprocity advantage* is an oxymoron for some people. It doesn't make sense to them because they define reciprocity as each party getting similar benefits—hence, no advantage. Current times urge some reflection on this assumption. Consider that disruptive innovation often occurs when two opposing concepts are put together and result in a new idea that shatters former assumptions. Sunny and rainy is a forecast for rainbows.

The ancient wisdom of reciprocity will be reborn in a digitally enhanced world of *And*. Transactions are choices made by businesses, usually in the interest of the intended customer. But transactions force the customer to choose among a small set of options offered to them. This is a world of *Or:* you can buy this *or* that. The future will be shaped by a wild array of external forces that will conspire to commoditize the world of Or in increasingly more extreme ways. Knock-off products will be created overnight—even faster than they are today—and competition over price alone will get fierce. Growth and ultimately success will depend on harnessing these forces and creating businesses together. The barriers to collaboration are falling just as pressures on price are increasing.

Reciprocity Will Scale Big

TEDx demonstrates the potential for *scalable* reciprocity to grow a good business and good will in ways that have never before been possible. In this book, we will show how companies such as IBM, Microsoft, Google, Apple, and Amazon are creating a new type of advantage. Reciprocity advantage must be done on a large scale to make a significant difference. We focus our examples on the point of view of the large company that already has scale but needs new growth, but small entrepreneurs are the likely partners. So, the roles may differ, but reciprocity advantage applies regardless of your size.

The world of the next ten years will best be characterized as volatile, uncertain, complex, and ambiguous (VUCA), which we talk about more in Part Two. But in spite of all the threats, it will also provide a window of opportunity—if we are smart enough to act now.[4] The VUCA World will demand reciprocity.

We have organized the book into three parts:

PART ONE
WHAT IS A RECIPROCITY ADVANTAGE?

- What is it?
- Understanding our model.

PART TWO
FUTURE FORCES THAT WILL DEMAND RECIPROCITY

- Why will it be important?
- Understanding that the future will be very different from the present—and how finding a reciprocity advantage can help you take advantage of the disruptions.

PART THREE
HOW TO DEVELOP YOUR OWN RECIPROCITY ADVANTAGE

- How can you do it?
- Finding new opportunities for growth.

This book introduces a reciprocity-based business model for creating growth that capitalizes on the future disruptions that are coming. We will challenge you to create your own reciprocity advantage.

Figure 2 introduces the model we have created for this book, a cycle from uncovering your *Right-of-Way* to *Partnering* to *Experiment to*

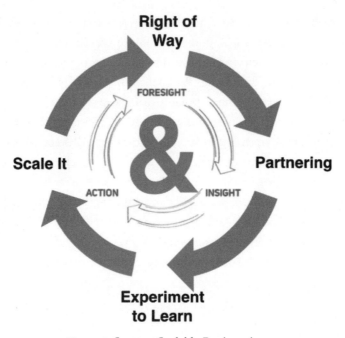

Figure 2: Steps to Scalable Reciprocity.

Learn and finally, when you are ready, to *Scale It.* This is an ongoing cycle, however, and it is unlikely to be a neat process. Certainly, it won't be linear.

Foresight, insight, and action will all play a role. Uncovering your right-of-way will involve rethinking your past with an eye toward your future.

All four steps summarized in Figure 2 must be mastered to create a reciprocity advantage. We start with right-of-way because the best reciprocity advantage will be grounded in a strong core business. However, we acknowledge that you may well run a lot of experiments and learn that you have an even better right-of-way to develop or that you have chosen the wrong partners. This is a cycle of learning, so expect to cycle round multiple times in order to develop your own reciprocity advantage. And to learn your way to the future will require partners.

Reciprocity-based business models will create new opportunities for high-margin businesses that can be much more profitable than traditional transactional businesses. The world of And can make the world a better place *and* make money. A reciprocity advantage is a chance to do good while also doing very well.

A reciprocity advantage is delicate to achieve and maintain. Go too wide, and you're a philanthropist. Go too narrow, and you'll be back doing transactions. Reciprocity is more than giving to get. Reciprocity is partnering for greater value for more players.

If you don't look out for your partners or if you don't have authenticity in your new business model, you'll just be doing clever marketing—not reciprocity.

Over the next decade, reciprocity advantage will become increasingly profitable and scalable in ways that are just becoming imaginable today. Future forces will disrupt your business, and that evidence is already visible. By providing many examples of companies that are already embracing the disruptions and by showing you the advantage of getting there early, this book will help you get started in creating your own reciprocity advantage.

Reciprocity on a Massive Scale

The four chapters in Part One introduce the four steps to reciprocity advantage. This four-step cycle will give you a new way to think about innovation and growth.

Chapter 1. Uncover your right-of-way—an existing platform where you already have permission to innovate with authenticity. Which of your assets have value for others and could also help you create complementary business growth? Essentially, what underutilized assets could you give away now that would yield greater value later?

Chapter 2. Find the best partners, ones who will allow you to accomplish what you could not do alone. Which partners will lower your risk, increase your innovation potential, and look out for you?

Chapter 3. Learn by experimenting. Give away assets intelligently in order to learn how to create value in new ways. The goal is to learn in an open, low-cost, and iterative way that allows for time to discover which questions to ask. How can you and your partners learn how to make money in new ways within your right-of-way?

Chapter 4. Scale it once you figure out what works, but keep it small until you are ready. The focus here is on how to make your new business big. Cloud-served supercomputing will be an amplifier for almost everything. When you are convinced that your business is **desirable**, **viable**, and **ownable**, you are ready to scale.

Following these four steps will help you uncover your right-of-way and create your reciprocity advantage, which will make extremely good business sense—given the external future forces of the next decade.

Creating new businesses is risky. Using your existing but under-utilized right-of-way to create a new business will lower your risk dramatically. You already own the assets you are sharing or giving away, and in most cases, you are not getting any value at present from these underutilized assets. If these assets can be unleashed to create new growth and capitalize on the disruptions that will occur in the near future, you can create a reciprocity advantage.

Reciprocity advantage will scale much faster if it is grounded in trust. James Fallows, in his book *More Like Us*, introduced the intriguing notion of a radius of trust:

> Except for psychopaths, everyone treats someone else decently. The question is how many people are classified as "us," deserving decent treatment, and how many are "them," who can be abused. When the radius of trust is small, the society is carved into tribes, castes, and clans. People are loyal to the handful of brothers inside the circle and may as well be at war with everyone else. The obligation to behave decently—and the expectation of decency in return—ends with family or friends. (*More Like Us*, p. 25)

Fallows was writing about trust in 1989. Building strong brands and strong businesses has always been an effort to build trust. What's changing is transparency.

In the past, companies could exert considerable control over their brand story through one-way broadcast media. In the future, control of corporate stories will be very difficult and transparency will be mandated. What people say about your brand will be much more important than what *you* say about your brand.

In a world of increasing global connectivity, the importance of trust will increase. Transparency will be required, while control of your own brand story will be increasingly difficult. If companies are not transparent, transparency will be forced upon them and forced transparency may well be unfair. Companies will need to embrace this loss of control but figure out ways to grow even when they do not have control. If you are not trustworthy, you will not grow in this world—at least not for long.

Figure 3: Step One toward Reciprocity Advantage.

CHAPTER 1

Reciprocity Right-of-Way

In which the complex notion of right-of-way is unpacked and put into play in search of growth and scale.

Right-of-way has multiple meanings. In law, it means a basic exclusivity where one person has permission to do something others cannot do. In California, Oregon, and some other states, pedestrians have the right-of-way over cars. According to Dictionary.com, right-of-way is defined as

1. a common law or statutory right granted to a vehicle, as an airplane or boat, to proceed ahead of another;
2. a path or route that may lawfully be used;
3. a right of passage, as over another's land;
4. the strip of land over which a power line, railway line, road, etc., extends.

Right-of-way is an unrealized opportunity space where you can create a new large-scale practice of exchanging with others for mutual benefit. Right-of-way is the space within which you can create your reciprocity advantage. Indeed, a reciprocity advantage becomes possible only within your right-of-way. For example, consider the evolution of IBM over the last 30 years.

IBM's Right-of-Way Reimagined

When Bob began his career in the 1970s, IBM (or Big Blue, as it was then called) had a very strong right-of-way selling big computers. Actually, big computers were the only computers then.

Institute for the Future, in those days, had Silicon Valley offices on Sand Hill Road (now referred to as the Wall Street of Silicon Valley) in Menlo Park, California, and IBM was IFTF's neighbor.

In the 1970s, IBM was a conservative company that was doing very well. IBM people were known for their conservative dress: usually dark blue suits. IBM's founder, Thomas J. Watson, purportedly said the reason IBM salesmen (they were almost all men at the time) wore blue suits, white shirts, and a red tie was because computers were so unreliable that the people who supported them had to look very reliable. Business casual came slowly to IBM, as did most everything else. Everything about IBM looked conservative. IBM offices looked conservative too.

One of the buildings IBM rented on Sand Hill Road, for example, was an especially fancy one that had been designed by an aggressively ostentatious company that eventually went bankrupt. IBM rented that fancy space anyway, but it just didn't fit the IBM image. Some of the individual executive offices had private patios, for example. When IBM moved in, they put filing cabinets in front of the patio doors in a futile attempt to make this overly fancy space feel like an IBM office. Those of us on Sand Hill Road at the time kidded that IBM's motto was "austerity . . . at any price."

Then the world changed, and IBM started on a path to uncover its unrealized right-of-way. This change also came slowly, but it has been dramatic and successful.

In an iconic Super Bowl commercial in 1984, Apple Computer introduced the Macintosh that was about to hit the market on January 24, 1984. In an only slightly veiled comparison of Big Blue to Big Brother from the George Orwell novel *1984*, the Apple commercial showed a female runner escaping gray guards and running up the aisle in a gray theatre with gray people sitting passively in rows watching a gray Big Brother lecture on a giant gray screen. The runner raced toward the front of the theatre and hurled a hammer through the screen. The shocked watchers gasped as they saw a *flash* just before a colorful message appeared on the screen announcing the new Apple Macintosh with this promise:

You'll see why 1984 won't be like *1984*.

As computers got smaller and more ubiquitous, IBM found it increasingly difficult to make money selling big computers—or even small computers, although they gave that a good try. IBM's right-of-way was disrupted by the very technology it was developing. The IBM story became a happy one, however, even though it had gloomy days. While IBM continued to sell to corporate clients, their hardware business became unprofitable. IBM smartly added a new source of growth: services. This was the first step in business reinvention done by CEO Lou Gerstner and followed up by Sam Palmisano with a move from an emphasis on products to an emphasis on services in support of products.

Services had always been part of IBM's business, but not as big a part and not as profitable a part as they were to become. IBM's services became a competitive advantage. The first reinvention of IBM was to understand service as a business in and of itself. This allowed the later decision to sell the computer hardware business and focus on other sources of growth. As business dress became more diversified, so did IBM's business offerings. Now they even study "Service Science" (short for Service Science, Management, and Engineering)[5] at their Almaden Research Center and other parts of the company. Just as IBM helped to seed and nurture the academic discipline of Computer Science, it is now seeding and nurturing Service Science.

IBM has become a vivid example of reciprocity at work. They call it "value co-creation." IBM uncovered an underutilized right-of-way that was linked to both its internal past and the external future. IBM created what we would call a reciprocity advantage.

IBM gradually realized that its core right-of-way is big data analytics and big data know-how. IBM is successfully engaged in big data management for customers around the world. IBM is now focused on custom software to manage and make sense out of your data. IBM has extensive big data analytic skills but needs very large data sets to apply those skills and draw business value from them. Since each challenge is different, IBM brings together a team that can add value for that particular situation.

IBM is creating a big data market with other people's data and then analyzing that data to achieve goals that neither IBM nor its clients could have done alone. IBM's three businesses are products, services, and software—but what it calls "software" looks like software solutions and software services to us. Through its study of services sciences, IBM is learning how to provide services in new ways through software and solutions. It is moving from what have become low-margin services to high-margin software services, some of which include IP licenses.

The Birth of Smarter Planet

Big Blue has reimagined itself as Smarter Planet, and it is grounded in the underutilized right-of-way that IBM uncovered. Grounded in its big data right-of-way, IBM is creating a new reciprocity advantage that capitalizes on the disruptions we discuss in Part Two of this book. IBM's big data expertise plus a customer's big data problem equals new businesses and new growth for IBM—plus new value for more players. IBM still has service businesses, but now they are creating new Smarter Planet businesses around the world. This is what Harvard Business School Professor Clayton Christenson recognizes as competing against nonconsumption—creating a business that had not been there before and therefore had no competitors. These new businesses are focused on big data problems that would not have been addressed if IBM didn't create new partnerships to solve them. IBM stakes out its right-of-way with these statements in its annual report:

- Big data is the planet's new natural resource.
- Advanced analytics enable us to mine it.

- Cloud computing is coming of age.
- Social and mobile create a new platform for work.[6]

And we would add: there will be new opportunities for new businesses, based on reciprocity advantage.

IBM is now reaching out to a wide range of big data problems, such as wind energy, customer retention, cancer treatment, and city operations. Essentially IBM is going out into the world and working with a wide range of difficult problems in search of opportunities to make sense out of complex data sets. It is going into spaces where nobody else has gone. As opportunities are discovered and prototyped, the Smart Planet branding gets applied with vigor.

Nobody, not even IBM, can make a smarter planet alone. Partners are needed, and IBM now has partners everywhere, of all sizes and with all kinds of offerings. Often, customers are also partners, and sometimes even competitors are partners. In Istanbul, for example, IBM worked with local governments, agencies, and companies to study traffic patterns by doing big data analytics on mobile phone traffic patterns. Based on these results, the city re-routed public transit patterns to better distribute the traffic flow and reduce congestion. IBM is co-creating a smarter planet with customers, cities, and regional economic development groups—but it is also becoming a very successful business.

IBM'S partners are sometimes unusual. When IBM introduced Watson, the challenge was in demonstrating what was then the world's most advanced computer with artificial intelligence that could understand free-form speech . How do you introduce a product that is so exotic and unusual? IBM chose to partner with the popular television show *Jeopardy!* At considerable risk, IBM entered Watson in a competition against two of the most successful human participants on *Jeopardy!* Fortunately for IBM, Watson won.

This limited partnership between IBM and *Jeopardy!* resulted in a mass understanding of what Watson could do, a mass understanding that played out over just two nights—but was rebroadcast in many forms afterward. Watson had a reputation overnight, which planted the seeds for the next big question: to whom could IBM give Watson so that it could have great value in creating a smarter planet and from whom IBM could make a considerable profit in providing services to support Watson? The answer is likely to be in health care, with a whole new set of partners—large and small.

As we were finishing this book, IBM announced that, about two years after its success on *Jeopardy!*, it is making Watson available as a development platform in the cloud to seed new software development applications on a worldwide scale.[7] The IBM Watson Developers Cloud began on November 14, 2013.

In Louisville, Kentucky, IBM partnered with a small startup company called Asthmapolis (now called Propeller Health) to create a healthier environment for kids with asthma. Asthmapolis has a GPS sensor inhaler that broadcasts the locations where the spray is used. IBM then does big data analysis to understand the parts of the city where the inhalers are used most frequently. This analysis gives the city an indicator of where pollution is most intense and harmful. The city then tries to get the problem corrected, but at least the kids can be re-routed around the areas of town where they will have the most trouble breathing. This kind of asymmetrical partnering (large companies with small companies or even individuals) is becoming much more possible now with the cloud, given all of the connections being drawn on a global scale.

IBM is still in the early days of building its new Smarter Planet businesses. It faces many challenges in its core businesses, but experimenting to create the future in addition to protecting the core is a robust, necessary strategy.

Ironically, since 1984, Apple has become more closed, while IBM has become aggressively more open. IBM is now one of four major players in the cloud (along with Google, Microsoft, and Amazon), and IBM is a major proponent of the shift from more closed to more open. IBM has opened its reciprocity right-of-way, while Apple has remained super-protective. Whether or not this more closed intellectual property strategy will work in the post–Steve Jobs era remains to be seen, but what is clear is that IBM has gone another way since that iconic 1984 commercial. Big Blue has transformed itself into Smarter Planet.

IBM'S RECIPROCITY ADVANTAGE IN SUMMARY

What right-of-way does IBM share with others? Big data know-how. For example, when IBM released Watson as a cloud service for developers, it began connecting app-builders with skilled professionals who could assist them in the specifics of creating a successful application for Watson in the cloud. IBM has committed more than 500 of its own subject-matter experts as part of this program, with expertise in areas like design, development, and research.[8]

Who are IBM's partners? Companies, cities, nonprofits, and others that have big data challenges partner with IBM, which looks for wicked problems and dilemmas that involve huge amounts of unstructured data. Those partners need to capture the data, analyze it, and create control strategies to make order out of chaos.

How did IBM experiment to learn? IBM experimented with a wide range of big data sources, such as stock exchanges, wind energy companies, customer retention studies, cancer researchers, and cities.

What assets does IBM give away in order to learn? Big data know-how in small chunks. It charges a lot for large chunks.

How did IBM scale? It seeks out the world's biggest problems that are occurring somewhere locally. Once the problem has been solved for an individual client, mass customized solutions can quickly be created for everyone else.

What is IBM's reciprocity advantage? The Smarter Planet Initiative has become synonymous with the IBM brand. Big data know-how embodied in software and services aimed at tackling the world's most wicked dilemmas.

So What?

In 2000, $3.3 billion of IBM's pre-tax profits came from hardware, $3.7 billion from services, and $2.6 billion from software, for a total of $9.6 billion. In 2012, software comprises $10.8 billion—larger than the whole company back in 2000—while hardware is still solid at $3.3 billion.[9] Imagine IBM if it had not embraced the new world.

CEO Virginia Rometty says in the 2012 annual report,

> To sustain an innovation model in our industry, a company must do more than accommodate major technology shifts.... [We are] becoming instrumented, interconnected and intelligent. Now the IT environment is moving from monolithic applications to dynamic services; from structured data at rest to unstructured data in motion; from PCs to unprecedented numbers and kinds of devices; from stable to unpredictable workloads; from static infra-structure to cloud services.[10]

Smarter Planet is becoming a key strategy for growth. Since 2005, IBM has acquired 33 companies to build its big data analytics capabilities, with a focus on helping customers turn massive volumes of unstructured data into valuable business information.

The same disruptions that disrupted IBM will disrupt all industries. IBM not only uncovered its right-of-way, it named and expressed it with great clarity: The Smarter Planet Initiative. Who doesn't want to create a smarter planet? And IBM has the credibility and trust to do it. IBM can argue authentically that it knows how to build a smarter planet. If you have a right-of-way that nobody trusts, it is not a right-of-way.

IBM people are building a smarter planet. This purpose-driving strategy is very motivational. IBM has become a much more open and creative place, all under the very motivational vision of the Smarter Planet Initiative. The Smarter Planet Initiative is motivating to IBM's own people, as well as to its customers. Language is very important. If you get the language right with regard to the future, the words draw you toward the future. If you get the language wrong, you fight it again and again. IBM got the language right. Smarter Planet is very clear and very aspirational.

IBM's reciprocity advantage comes from a creative mix of openness, intellectual property, and services. Other competitors offer big data services, but it is difficult for them to compete with IBM in the space that IBM has defined as Smarter Planet.

The Historic Right-of-Way Story

The idea of right-of-way goes way back. The history of Silicon Valley, where both Bob and Karl live, is inextricably linked to railroads. Stanford University's full name is the Leland Stanford Junior University, named after the son of the founder of the Union Pacific Railroad. You can see a golden spike in the university's museum. The transcontinental railroad was cutting-edge technology for its day when finished in 1869. Suddenly it became possible to travel or send goods across the continent in what, at the time, was amazing speed.

The railroad developed into the major growth industry of the late nineteenth century. But how often do you ride a long-distance train today? In dense urban areas we still use commuter trains, but planes, trucks, and cars have now replaced the bulk of the transportation—and disrupted the trains business.

As much as the railroad companies missed the transition from trains to modes of transportation that did not require rails, the big miss was not foreseeing the potential that arose from thinking differently about the land that was under and above the rails. The land *under* the tracks is the classic right-of-way. But *above* those tracks, invisible in plain view, was a right-of-way that the railroads owned but completely missed: communications.

The railroads already had the land underneath their trains when the telegraph developers approached them and wanted to string wires above the tracks. To the railroads, this new telegraph technology offered the promise of reducing their old cost structure. With the telegraph, the railroads could know where all their trains were, for free.

All that the trains got from the telegraph, however, was an incremental cost reduction in their old business that was about to be disrupted. They did use the telegraph to make the trains run better.

With the telegraph they could know whenever their trains entered a station. This enormous logistics benefit allowed them to easily adopt the telegraph as a tool for making their current business better.

It was a windfall to the railroads at the time, but years later we all now realize that the railroads missed claiming most of the benefits from their own right-of-way. The railroads completely missed the communications revolution—which turned out to be even more important than railroads.

The railroads owned the land over and underneath their tracks. Long before the development of airplanes and trucks—which would technologically disrupt the railroads—the space above their tracks was available for a new kind of business: communication.

If they had seen the potential for the telegraph to be a business in its own right as complementary to riding a train, today we might be talking on Union Pacific phones rather than AT&T or Verizon. They had the physical right-of-way in their land and used it only to grow their core business. Recall that there was no monopoly regulation in those days to constrain them.

The railroad companies probably never would have been great managers in the development of telecommunications. But they never had to become great telecommunications managers. They only needed to partner with others, offering their land rights to create a deal with those who could create that new business and then prosper together. Eventually, as it caught on, they would have the inside track on investing more deeply or even buying out their partners.

It seems clear in retrospect that the people who ran the railroads were train people with limited points of view. They failed to see the value of the space *over* their own tracks; they failed to see their own right-of-way. As Tim Brown, CEO of the design firm IDEO, observed, they loved their trains too much.

Uncovering your own right-of-way involves understanding what the railroads never did learn, that every company is really in three businesses.

Product—Railroads that move people and goods.

Service—Transportation, any way that moves people or goods *en masse.*

Experience—Communications, any way to get the benefit of travel without physical movement. (The railroads' missed reciprocity advantage.)

Chapter 9 shows you how you can determine your three industries—your equivalent to trains, transportation, and communications. Companies must defend those businesses and make the difficult transition from one to another (e.g., trains to transportation to communications) in order to avoid becoming obsolete. Your equivalent of a communications business is the most likely place you will discover the potential for explosive growth.

Each business has the potential to create massively scalable reciprocity if it can uncover its right-of-way for complementary growth. Land for the railroads was a physical right-of-way, embodied in the air over the tracks. But right-of-way can include products, services, and experiences. For TED, it is the eighteen-minute speech format and TEDx-in-a-Box. For IBM's Smarter Planet Initiative, it is IBM's expertise in managing large data sets that is turned into a search for new data sets to manage.

Uncovering your right-of-way is the first step to creating a reciprocity advantage. Then you look for the right partner who can help you do what you cannot do alone.

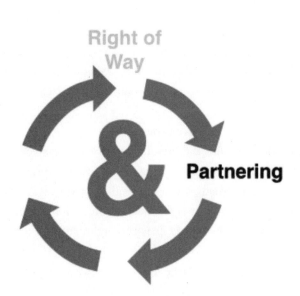

Figure 4: Step Two toward
Reciprocity Advantage.

CHAPTER 2

Partnering to Do What You Can't Do Alone

In which partnering, collaboration, and teaming
are reimagined on a global scale.

Microsoft Kinect was introduced in December of 2010. Within days of its release, it was hacked. Even worse for Microsoft, a new website came alive that solicited and shared illegal Kinect hacks globally.

Stunned Microsoft lawyers let these intellectual property violations happen for a few days and then announced that they would sue anyone who hacked the Kinect platform. In defiance of Microsoft's legal threat, a prize was offered for the best hack of the Kinect platform.

Two months later, Microsoft opened the Kinect platform with an act of involuntary reciprocity that was truly remarkable and even inspiring. Microsoft discovered its reciprocity advantage after its right-of-way was exposed and forced open. A bunch of hackers discovered Microsoft's underutilized right-of-way for them. The Kinect was not just a new gaming platform. The Microsoft right-of-way embedded in Kinect was much broader: 3D motion-sensing hardware and software—a new way to interact with computers. The Microsoft Kinect right-of-way now reaches far beyond video gaming. Kinect was the first general-purpose, low-cost gestural interface for computers. Microsoft showed great agility in response to this attack on its intellectual property by flipping the negatives into positives. Microsoft eventually embraced the hackers and uncovered a wider right-of-way that was not visible until the hackers broke into it.

It was reasonable to try to protect the Kinect IP because to Microsoft at the time, Kinect was perceived only as a gaming platform. After realizing that it was impossible to protect its IP, Microsoft quickly pivoted toward finding partners to bring the Kinect platform into other sectors, beyond gaming. It was smart to try to protect its intellectual property, but it was brilliant to realize that opening the platform would yield much more value. Besides, it could not be protected anyway. Microsoft turned a big problem into an even bigger opportunity.

Microsoft Kinect is a wonderful gestural interface device originally created for the Xbox 360. Kinect allows people to interact with computers simply by moving their bodies and speaking. It is a very sophisticated 3D rendering and yet very easy to use. When it was first introduced, it was positioned as a gaming platform that allowed people to play games with their bodies, like the Wii but without having to hold a wand as you play.

MICROSOFT KINECT'S RECIPROCITY ADVANTAGE IN SUMMARY

What right-of-way was Microsoft Kinect forced to share with others? The Kinect platform with its 3D motion-sensing hardware and software.

Who are Kinect's partners? The people who at first tried to hack them and who Microsoft at first tried to sue, as well as others who Microsoft has now attracted intentionally.

How did Kinect experiment to learn? It learned from hackers who experimented with Kinect, some in the early days without Microsoft's permission. Microsoft was smart enough to learn from this experience, accept that it could not control Kinect, open the Kinect platform, and encourage much wider experimentation to create new gestural computing applications and businesses. Even though Microsoft lost control, it gained power in the marketplace.

What assets does Kinect give away in order to learn? Users and entrepreneurs are given the right to use the Kinect platform and create new applications or to start new businesses.

How did Microsoft Kinect scale? It supports Kinecthack.com and other hacker sites that curate new ideas, share hacks, and spread the use of Kinect. This puts Microsoft on the exploding leading edge of gestural computing. One day we expect to see Microsoft acquire some of these entrepreneurial businesses as the new field matures. But for now, it must keep enabling the growth that was originally discouraged.

What is Microsoft Kinect's reciprocity advantage? Kinect is a foundation of and tool for gestural computing businesses.

So What?

Microsoft is not just making money from selling Kinect boxes. It now has a new profitable business growth engine that extends way beyond gaming. Microsoft Kinect is embracing the opportunity to lead the way in gestural interfaces of any kind, not just for gaming. Microsoft reports that the Kinect for Windows software development kit (SDK) has been downloaded more than half a million times, and Kinect for Windows sensors are available in 39 markets around the world. Here's how Microsoft expresses this commitment now: "With Kinect for Windows, businesses and developers can create a new class of touch-free applications that give people the ability to interact naturally with computers by simply gesturing and speaking. What can a computer do if you give it eyes, ears, and the capacity to use them?"[11]

By developing its reciprocity advantage—even if involuntarily—Microsoft is now learning new ways to make money from Kinect across a wide range of industries. By giving up control, Microsoft broadened the Kinect brand and the Microsoft brand. Microsoft is now challenging businesses and developers to create a new genre of gestural applications. Businesses from startups to Fortune 500 companies are using Kinect to develop immersive experiences of widely varied sorts. The Kinect software developer kit has been downloaded millions of times in many countries. Microsoft is working with the hackers and others in very creative ways to create new businesses.

One of the major disruptions in the future will be the increasing difficulty of protecting intellectual property. For some, they will uncover their own reciprocity advantage only after more protective strategies fail. Even if you want to protect your intellectual property—to protect your right-of-way—you may be forced to open up anyway. Reciprocity may not come naturally. Even companies who try to protect their intellectual property may be forced to partner and forced into finding a new reciprocity advantage. Now in Silicon Valley, most conversations about intellectual property have at least one lawyer asking if there could be more business value in giving it away in smart ways, rather than trying to lock it up.

Judge Alex Kozinski of the Ninth Circuit Court of Appeals in California commented, "Intellectual property rights are like children: cling to them too closely and you may lose them forever."[12]

Ideas are also like children: cling to them too closely and you will lose them forever. Nevertheless, reaching out to others—potential partners and potential customers—will become increasingly possible and increasingly necessary.

Partnering to Reduce Food Safety Risk

The Global Food Safety Initiative (GFSI) is an example of global partnering with an extremely wide reach across companies. GFSI began as a response to a series of food safety crises around the year 2000. Here is the way that the GFSI describes the environment that created this need:

> Back in 2000, food safety was a top of mind issue for companies due to several high-profile recalls, quarantines and negative publicity about the food industry. There was also extensive audit fatigue through the industry, as retailers performed inspections or audits themselves or asked a third party to do this on their behalf. These

were often carried out against food safety schemes that lacked international certification and accreditation, resulting in incomparable auditing results.[13]

Up to that point, players up and down the food chain had their own approach to food safety. Some players were better at food safety than others, but the food supply chain is interlinking, so food safety mistakes can multiply rapidly. Also, the consumers of food often blame food safety mistakes on companies that had nothing to do with the problem. A bird flu scare in China can cause a consumer in Illinois to eat something other than chicken—even if there is no rational argument for doing that.

McDonald's, one of GFSI's early board members, has found that partnering was a way to engage positively with the growing numbers of people who are concerned about food safety. In the minds of many people, McDonald's has a right-of-way with regard to food safety and health. McDonald's restaurants are very clean and known for high food safety standards. In emerging markets where food safety is more of a concern, the McDonald's brand is perceived as a safe place to eat. Yet, food safety is a problem that McDonald's cannot deal with alone. If a food scare happens around chicken, for example, many people will stop eating McDonald's Chicken McNuggets—even if McDonald's is not at fault and even if the scare has nothing to do with them.

In February of 2008, Walmart announced that all of its private (store) brand suppliers and some of their national brand suppliers would be required to become certified based on one of the GFSI standards. An independent study published in the *Journal of Food Protection* in 2012 found that adoption of GFSI standards resulted in fewer safety audits—on the average one less per year, at considerable cost savings. Another positive outcome from GFSI was an increase in employee food safety training.[14]

GFSI is a nonprofit business that allows all competitors in the food industry to compete at a higher level. More important, GFSI reduces the risks of food safety scares for consumers and for suppliers up and down the food chain.

GFSI'S RECIPROCITY ADVANTAGE IN SUMMARY

What right-of-way has the GFSI created to share with others? Each company shares its science, standards, and practices in food safety.

Who are GFSI's partners? Anyone involved at any stage in the food supply cycle.

How did GFSI experiment to learn? It tried many different approaches in its early days and has now evolved to be a global brand—expanding up and down the food chain. They began with benchmarking on a global scale to look for opportunities that would add new value by working together to improve food safety as well as opportunities to create new business value.

What assets do member companies and GFSI give away? Food safety standards, science, and techniques, plus their time to create the standards.

How did GFSI scale? GFSI now sponsors a wide range of events for food safety professionals internationally in programs and standards—as well as ways of responding quickly to food safety crises.

What is GFSI's reciprocity advantage? As the founders say, "Food safety is not a competitive advantage." GFSI allows its members to achieve their own competitive advantage in areas other than food safety. A strong, consistent approach to food safety assurance creates a low-cost solution that allows everyone to focus on higher order benefits.

So What?

GFSI recently commissioned the first study by an independent research group to help assess the initiative to date. The researchers concluded that GFSI has contributed significantly with the following benefits:

- A more effective food safety system and enhanced ability to produce safe food

- Enhanced compliance with regulators, with a reduction in the number of notifications and product recalls
- Improvements in the culture of food safety and the human behaviors that are required[15]

GFSI is a better way to deliver food safety. GFSI lowers the cost of food safety while also allowing members to focus on delighting their customers and competing at a higher level.

GFSI encourages companies of all sizes anywhere in the world to partner for overall food safety. GFSI is a nonprofit reciprocity-advantage business that increases the profit for each member company by lowering the risk of costly safety and health mistakes. Lowering this risk allows companies to focus on creating better products and more successful businesses.

GFSI is massive reciprocity on a global scale. Companies are giving away their expertise in food safety in order to compete at a higher level on the assumption that all the food will be safe. Today's Internet and tomorrow's cloud will make it possible for ever-larger numbers of partners to participate in GFSI. When a food safety crisis breaks out, as it certainly will, this global connectivity brings together the resources to respond much more quickly and effectively. The GFSI partners assert, "Food safety is not a competitive advantage." GFSI offers a reciprocity advantage to its member companies. By sharing its food safety expertise, it lowers its overall risks in the face of food safety scares.

Individual companies—like McDonald's, Cargill, Tesco, and many others—were able to team with other food companies to strengthen the Global Food Safety Initiative—an excellent example of reciprocity advantage that leverages right-of-way through partnering. By combining with other companies, a shared network of trust and right-of-way around global food safety was created. GFSI, however, can help individual members widen their right-of-way and lower their risks.

New Ways to Partner on a Global Scale

In the past, it was just easier to partner with those who were close to you geographically. And besides, partnerships were—in most industries—quite limited and viewed skeptically. There were many suppliers and vendors in transactional relationships, but few true partners for most corporations. Transactions still dominate and they will continue to be important. Now, however, transactions are skewing toward commoditization and competition based on price. So much of today's Internet is focused on finding the lowest price for something.

Connectivity has grown dramatically, and potential partners can come from anywhere. In a VUCA World, partnerships will be hedges against risk, but they will also be more attractive ways to innovate and grow scale. Innovation in the cloud will focus on value, not just price. The greatest value and the largest margins will come from services and experiences that link to products, not just on selling for the lowest price. Price-based competition will be cutthroat and unattractive. Value-based partnerships will be the key to growth, scalability, and profitability. Larger social value, beyond just transactional value, will become possible on a much grander scale.

When TED decided to allow anyone to organize a TEDx conference, it took a risk, reaching out to a wide range of potential partners around the world. TED was fishing for partners with very attractive bait: "Ideas Worth Spreading." It was a risk worth taking when TEDx spread around the world and went viral. TEDx also helped identify and evaluate potential partners for growing the TED brand.

What if the railroads had viewed the telegraph companies as potential partners to explore the emerging communications space, instead of seeing their proposal as a narrow business transaction? Of course, the times were different, and those who created the railroad industry had their own interests that blinded them to the virtues of partnerships in the ways we can imagine them now.

As Internet connectivity expands, new potential partners become available who were simply not reachable before. The biggest change will happen in the developing world, as access opens for many who have been previously excluded. Marginalized communities in all countries of the globe will be able to take advantage of connectivity in ways that have never before been possible. Many new potential partners will become available.

In the future, it will be easier to bring partners together to create new economic value. Partners, of course, must demonstrate their worth to each other and in the marketplace over time. The best partners will demonstrate their worth by looking out for one another. By looking out for one another, they will also be protecting themselves over time. Mandatory transparency will change the rules for engagement.

New partnerships will become possible through the cloud. The medium of the cloud is opening to many more potential partners. Internet domains, for example, are already emerging to support more local languages.

At the network level, the body responsible for overseeing the architecture of the web, ICANN, has led this development with the approval for the creation of top-level domains in local languages. This means that as country-level markets evolve, the domain registration patterns will likely tend to shift toward these and away from the dot-com top-level domain that is most common today. The main reason for this is that the web has already become a major advertising and sales platform for businesses, and much of their commerce is local. Because localized top-level domains are by nature self-identifying, their business is linked with the country. Western preferences will no longer be the default standard.

Partnerships are basic to creating your reciprocity advantage, and partnerships will be possible on a scale never before imaginable. Asymmetrical partnering, where one partner is much larger than the other, will become increasingly possible because anyone can link to anyone else through the cloud. Non-obvious partners will become more common. Partnerships will not be predetermined. Everyone will need to learn how to fish for partners efficiently and effectively. It will be easier to find partners, however, within established networks of trust.

Companies Want Good Partners—
for Good Reasons

Already, companies are seeing the need to re-think partnering. General Electric and Strategy One did a recent survey of over 3,000 executives from 25 countries that found that the great majority of executives believe they could innovate better by partnering than by working on their own.[16] Even more impressive, most have actually partnered already. Large company executives see small businesses and individuals as the best potential partners. These asymmetrical partnerships seem most promising—and the means for identifying and drawing connections are improving dramatically in the world of hyper-connectivity.

Of course, good companies develop strong relationships with those who supply the essential goods and services along the entire value chain. But these "partnerships" are often transactional and inherently one-sided. We're talking about partnering in a much more profound sense, to create something new that you could not do alone. Your partner will bring skills and resources to take your new business into places where you could not go alone.

Equal partnership in the reciprocity advantage is critical to creating the new business. This all-in collaboration is what we have always heard of in the founding of great companies. Hewlett needed Packard. Procter needed Gamble. Jobs needed Wozniak. You will need your complementary partner or partners. You don't have to like these partners, but you do need to trust them.

In the future, some of the most interesting partnerships will be asymmetrical: very big companies partnering with very small companies—or even with individuals. Your partner might be a single inventor, or it might be lead users from around the world.

What would your company love to do, but could not do without a good partner that is unlike you? What does your right-of-way give you permission to do with others, but that you are not yet doing and could not do alone?

You will have to experiment to learn how to answer these questions and to create your reciprocity advantage.

CHAPTER 3

Experimenting to Learn: How to Make Money in New Ways

In which hundreds of open prototypes are used to create reciprocity advantage.

The old train station in Kansas City is a beautiful building, but there aren't many trains anymore. Kansas City used to be a major stop for the train lines going west and east. The trains connected Kansas City to the world, and in those days, Kansas City was very connected. Entire businesses were built around the Kansas City train station. As train travel became less important, most of those businesses went elsewhere or died.

On March 30, 2011, Google announced that it had selected Kansas City as the first community in its new high-speed digital network. More than 1,100 communities applied, but Kansas City won the competition—at least partially because the city had become so unconnected in 2011.

To Kansas City, Google Fiber looked like the trains were coming back in a new digital form. Google Fiber brought new hope for connectivity.

To Google, Kansas City looked like an unusual chance to experiment to learn about the impacts of overnight super digital bandwidth upon a city that was decidedly disconnected and largely non-digital.

When the Google Fiber initiative began, Google was fishing for

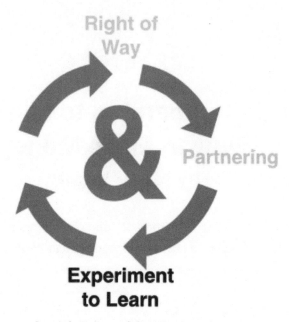

Figure 5: Step Three toward Reciprocity Advantage.

partners. Google Fiber offered a hundredfold increase in bandwidth, all at once. Google Fiber was not a grant or a gift; it was an investment in scalable reciprocity. Google is seeking a reciprocity advantage. It is important that Google doesn't know yet what gain it will receive. It is taking a risk that, in the long run, Google will receive value and growth. Kansas City stands to benefit as well, along with a wide array of new businesses.

Subscribers have to pay for services through the network (although there is a free broadband Internet service), but the extreme bandwidth would not have been available in Kansas City for years were it not for Google. Google's gift to Kansas City was early access to extreme bandwidth, just like the railroads gave Kansas City early access to railroad commerce.

Google, as best we can tell, had little idea how Kansas City businesses, schools, nonprofits, government agencies, and individual people would use the radically increased bandwidth. Google knew it could not do this alone, so it began experimenting—first by selecting Kansas City from among a wide range of other metropolitan areas and then by opening an incredibly rich zone of experimentation. Now, Kansas City is booming with hackers and makers, all searching for new models of innovation that benefit from the great increase in bandwidth. We know market research companies that are buying houses in Kansas City just to tune into the experimentation that is happening.

Most of these experiments were not just technology tests; they were partnership tests. Kansas City has become a speed-dating hot zone for bandwidth partnerships. Prototype, listen, learn.

GOOGLE FIBER'S RECIPROCITY ADVANTAGE IN SUMMARY

What right-of-way does Google share with others? Google Fiber provides wide bandwidth capabilities that would not otherwise have been available in Kansas City for a long time.

Who are Google's partners? The citizens of Kansas City and any entrepreneur or company that wants to experiment in the high-speed future Google is creating.

How does Google experiment to learn? Google puts the platforms out there and seeds experimentation—without knowing what will happen. Google does not control what happens on their platforms. Others do most of the experimentation, and Google collects data to learn from it.

What assets does Google give away in order to learn? Google gives access to Google Fiber and early access to platforms for digital prototyping on very large scales.

How did Google Fiber scale? Google Fiber will take whatever works in this modern version of a classic test-market city and expand it globally. Anyone who runs a test of his or her new idea in Kansas City will also be able to see the future and expand, following Google's expansion. Google uses the cloud. Others make their own investments in the hope that they will be amplified through Google Fiber and the cloud.

What is Google's reciprocity advantage? Google Fiber allows Google to see the future sooner by removing the speed limitations and collecting usage data on all new Google or competitive platforms. Google has a basic motivation to create collaborative platforms that can be used by Google and others to create reciprocity advantages.

So What?

In early 2014, Google announced that Google Fiber would be expanded to 34 cities. Clearly, the experiment is working. "The future of the Internet will be built on gigabit speeds," said Google Fiber General Manager Kevin Lo in an interview. "We're going to do our part to help move the web forward."[17] Google is experimenting in places like Kansas City to learn the benefits of ultra-fast speeds. Google Fiber has already become an independent growth engine for Google—and its partners. Google wants to see the future faster and realizes it can't do that alone.

Google has a similar challenge to IBM's in that it is reaching out into the world to seek out situations where it can add value. It is learning how to grow and make money in new ways.

In addition to Google Fiber, there are similar efforts under way at Google in other fields. IBM has Smarter Planet; Google has Google Fiber, Google Car, or Google Anything. For example, Google Earth Engine is providing a platform for analyzing and scaling Google Earth data from many diverse sources. The first efforts are to track global deforestation.

Google Car is exploring driverless vehicles. In the Bay Area, we have seen the Google Car on our highways for several years now—with no accidents (except for one that happened when the human was driving). Certainly, every major car company also has autonomous vehicle experiments going on, but Google has created its own platform for experimentation.

Google Glass is a wearable computer that can shoot pictures or video, make and receive calls and texts, and access the Internet. The first-generation prototype has voice control and a touch-sensitive temple plate on the glasses. Google Glass has obvious applications for people with disabilities, but it is also a big step toward a graceful virtual overlay on the physical world. There was so much interest in Google Glass that Google requested proposals from people who wanted the right to buy early prototypes. Again, Google is experimenting to learn.

Experimenting to Learn Will Get Smarter and Faster

In their current business, most companies already do prototyping. They make models of the product or service and share it with potential customers and then take the best versions to management to gain alignment to the new direction. The range of prototypes is bound by the limits of the existing business. This type of testing is done to prove you are right before going to market.

The market for your reciprocity advantage business probably doesn't exist yet. Therefore, you will need to prototype more broadly than you ever have before. To learn about the future, you will need to be able to produce thousands of prototypes rapidly and at low cost. This skill is called *design thinking* and is practiced by companies such as IDEO, the Silicon Valley innovation firm that created the Apple mouse and many other everyday objects we all take for granted. Common language in the design community is to refer to these efforts as *low resolution prototypes.*

You will have to experiment to learn and do so with your partners in order to find your reciprocity advantage. Hundreds or thousands of low-resolution prototypes are needed to find the reciprocity advantage that will add onto your core business in complementary ways without cannibalizing it.

In Kansas City, Google is demonstrating new ways to experiment, new ways to learn. The practices of experimenting to learn will disrupt business development and market research. Traditional market research has focused on surveys using stratified random samples of the population you are interested in reaching. The new market research is less controlled and more open. To learn, you reach out through the web to explore, as TED did with online TED Talks and the TEDx conferences.

You have to learn how to give up control in order to derive insights and to gain power.

Rapid prototyping is the ability to create quick, early versions of innovations, with the expectation that later success will require early failures.[18] Our favorite call for rapid prototyping has echoed around P&G for years, although it was sometimes hard to execute around: "Fail early, fail often, and fail cheaply!"

In Silicon Valley, if you haven't failed, you are perceived as not having taken enough risks. Indeed, when Alan Kay was at Xerox PARC, he was known for saying that the purpose of research is to fail, but to fail in an interesting way.

At IDEO, there are prototypes everywhere—most of which didn't make it anywhere near the marketplace. When you begin an industrial design project at IDEO, the assumption is that you will make the first prototype on the first day of the project and it will fail, but the focus is on learning from failure. Experimenting to learn.

Rapid prototyping is getting smarter and faster. When TED decided to open its brand, it began by posting free videos from TED Talks. How did the people at TED know this approach would work? They didn't. Rather, they conducted cheap, fast experiments and learned their way to success. TED Talks existed as recordings and were routinely sent to the attendees following each conference. Since the market for TED talks was unknowable, the breakthrough question was, How cheaply can we put them online? The breakthrough question was *not*, How much money can we make putting them online? Cheap experiments allow you to find a profitable business model.

Initially six videos of TED Talks were put online, and they had three million views within a year. From this in-market prototype, they were able to expand. After seven years, the growth curve of viewing remained exponential, surpassing one billion. Most organizations would debate the fate of their brand and the size of the market for such a monumental change in their business.

The future will be created with smart, fast, cheap experiments in the real world.

TechShop: A Place to Experiment and Learn

TechShop is like a gymnasium for makers. For a monthly fee, members get access to state-of-the-art tools of all varieties. It is a membership-based, do-it-yourself maker space. Actually, we see it as more of a do-it-*ourselves* space, since so much of the TechShop use is group or community oriented. Makers of all kinds use TechShop—entrepreneurs, craftspeople, artists, hobbyists, and people who just like to hang with makers.

TechShop was a spinoff of the MakerFaire, *Make* magazine's extravaganza for makers that draws more than 100,000 people over a weekend every spring in the Bay Area.

TechShop was also a spinoff of the popular TV show *MythBusters*. Jim Newton, the TechShop founder, was the former chief scientist on the show, which takes commonly held beliefs about science, life, and common sense, and puts them to the test—using applied science and clever engineering. The result is down-to-earth science and fascinating entertainment. Jim Newton is a master maker and teacher. He loves to make and help others make. Bob took the CEO of a major corporation to visit the first TechShop, and Jim went along on the tour. When they got to a room where the makers share their tools, Jim was drawn to a new set of tools he had not seen before. Ten minutes later, in another room, Bob noticed that Jim was missing. He was still back there playing with his new tools. Even hosting an important CEO could not distract him from his love of making. Love of making is in the air at any TechShop. In our experience, you cannot visit a TechShop without coming away feeling infused with positive maker spirit.

Makers are not new. The maker instinct is an ancient need that all people have to make and grow things. What's new is the ability to create and amplify communities of makers. Makers are all about experimenting to learn.

TechShop is a radical maker amplifier that is based on the principles of reciprocity. TechShop gives access to tools that can be shared and provides a space for makers to share ideas and build new businesses. Ford Motor Company, for example, has a TechShop adjacent to its campus in Dearborn, Michigan, where there are two conspicuous telephones: one goes directly to the U.S. Patent Office; the other, to Ford's innovation office. The phones are rarely used, but they symbolize the spirit of TechShop: anyone can make the future; anyone can make a new business.

Mark Hatch, the CEO of TechShop, has written the definitive book on the maker movement as expressed through TechShop and other similar adventures. The tone of the book is characterized by what he calls the "Maker Movement Manifesto," which is expressed in the following core concepts:

Make	Learn	Participate
Share	Tool up	Support
Give	Play	Change

Fittingly, the manifesto ends with the following charge: "In the spirit of making, I strongly suggest that you take this manifesto, make changes to it, and make it your own. That is the point of making."[19] These core concepts are essential in experimenting to learn.

The Maker Movement Manifesto is rooted in reciprocity (share, give, participate, support), with an emphasis on experimenting to learn (make, learn, tool up, play, change).

TechShop provides a place for others to experiment and learn at a very low cost. Instead of having your own machine shop or prototyping laboratory, you can join a TechShop and get access to state-of-the-art tools for almost nothing. TechShop is a shared space for rapid prototyping. It is heaven for hackers. Most important, TechShop offers a community of makers who learn from and support each other.

Square, for example, created prototypes of its plug-in device for processing credit card transactions on a smart phone at the first TechShop in Menlo Park, California. It began as a maker project, but it scaled to a successful company with an intriguing product. The hope of a prototype becoming a product hangs in the air at TechShop, although their members are a wild mix of entrepreneurs, artists, hobbyists, and just people who like to make stuff.

Experimenting to learn rarely happens alone. In most cases, the more people who get involved, the faster the learning. One very important way to get more people involved is to make it fun.

Gaming: A Breakthrough for Experimenting to Learn

Gaming is meaningful engagement. Our favorite definition of gaming is this:

emotionally enhanced attention

FoldIt is a massive online gaming environment developed at the University of Washington. FoldIt engages with people from all around the world who volunteer to play a game that involves folding proteins and other scientific tasks that nontechnical people can do while also contributing to things that are difficult for scientists to do on a large scale. It has been used to contribute to research projects and to search for cures for specific diseases. In some cases, the crowd playing FoldIt games has contributed to new research findings and even journal publications with thousands of "authors." FoldIt is socially important gaming that is also fun to play. FoldIt is scalable reciprocity in both individual and organizational ways. Players give their time and energy in exchange for fun and the knowledge that they are contributing to a larger scientific and human good. FoldIt allows many people to learn by experimenting together. Earlier efforts, such as those by SETI, the Search for Extraterrestrial Intelligence, have shared underutilized computational resources for social good like this, but FoldIt is engaging underutilized intellectual resources—with a touch of fun.

Another example is the UCLA BioGames Project, which has used massive online gaming to address specific problems of diagnosing malaria in sub-Saharan Africa. When the project started, trained pathologists needed to study 300 different fields of view from a red blood cell sample in order to come up with an accurate diagnosis. The

BioGames prototype worked by aggregating the opinions of hundreds of nonexpert online gamers to diagnose malaria just as accurately as a trained pathologist on site. Game participants are challenged by visual puzzles that they arrange and rearrange. Through clever game design, the BioGames Project has been able to create engaging experiences that are both fun and scientifically accurate.

Since it is often very difficult to get a trained pathologist on site at the right time, the potential for online gaming is attractive indeed. Consider how something like FoldIt or BioGames could be used to experiment together, with input from an online crowd of gamers. Gaming is an accelerated way to experiment to learn, but the games must be engaging and the experience rewarding.

The prototypes for both FoldIt and the BioGames malaria diagnostics are grounded in a spirit of reciprocity. They ask people to give in order to contribute to a higher purpose. Imagine how games could be expanded to tap into more complex reciprocity-based business models.

Reciprocity and gaming will grow together. There is an inherent give-and-take to most games. Zero-sum games have clear winners and losers. Many games, however, have more than one winner and more than one way to win. Gameful engagement is a much broader concept. Gameful engagement is emotion-laden attention.

Simulation and gaming will provide low-risk opportunities to experiment and learn.

The psychological principles of gaming are powerful. There has been talk of how they might be applied to situations ranging from workplace settings to civic engagement. Workplace applications are potentially limitless. Many organizations already rely on elements of games to engender constructive competition, create team spirit, make team activities more fun, and generally add levity to the workday. Yet, today's sales competitions will pale in comparison to the gameful engagement tools available to augment in the future. It should be noted that this increased engagement does not come at the expense of productivity but is rather the very driver of it. As Stanford professor Byron Reeves observes: "Fun is not the enemy of work."[20]

By adding a touch of fun, it will be possible to get more people engaged in experimenting to learn.

In *Leaders Make the Future*, Bob talks about the leadership skill he calls Immersive Learning Ability, which is the "ability to immerse yourself in unfamiliar environments, to learn from them in a first-person way." A range of gameful engagement experiences will get increasingly richer in the future, including these:

- Simulations of reality
- Alternate reality games
- 3D immersive environments
- Role-play simulations
- Immersive scenarios or case studies
- Theatrical improvisation[21]

Rapid prototyping and gaming are already providing impressive ways to learn by experimenting together—on a very large scale. Considering that hundreds or even thousands of prototypes are going on *simultaneously*, not sequentially, it is clear that companies won't be able to control what's going on. *Make* magazine, the guiding source of the maker movement, has the following motto: "If you can't open it, you don't own it."[22] Companies must let people inside their products if they are going to prototype the next generation of what is possible. Companies must lose some control in order to gain the next advantage. Companies must give in order to get people engaged and in order to learn.

The challenge is how to craft giveaways that inspire contributions to a commons (a shared asset) that builds your brand and that contributes to new markets. Many rapid-fire open prototypes will be the best way to learn.

Your core business is where you make money now. Your reciprocity advantage will be different, and yet it needs to be 100 percent complementary with your core business. You will have to give up control in order to experiment and learn how to create your reciprocity advantage. Once you've prototyped it and shown that it can work, you will be ready to scale.

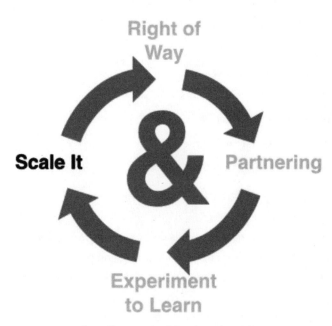

Figure 6: Step Four toward Reciprocity Advantage.

CHAPTER 4

Amplifying to Create Scale

In which the emphasis shifts from innovation to propagation.

———

The problem is not the pace of innovation.
The problem is the pace of propagation.

DANIEL BEN-HORIN,
Founder of TechSoup Global

———

Daniel Ben-Horin wrote an article provocatively entitled "Innovation Obsession Disorder." He argues, "We need a new consensus that propagation is as important as innovation."[23]

In some sense, innovation is the easy part. Humans innovate quite naturally, but propagation is really hard and can be quite unnatural. Ben-Horin, quite an innovator himself, has become a prophet for propagation, a prophet for scaling.

Reciprocity advantage, thanks to digital technology, will become much more practical over the next decade. While traditional platforms will not go away overnight, their position in the infrastructure of innovation will shift markedly as the cloud comes to life. Organizations need to explore these dynamics before they find themselves disrupted by them.

Apple's Ironic Reciprocity Advantage

Consider the reciprocity advantage that Apple created with its App Store—and the scalability amplifier that it has become. For many people, Apple is practicing anything but reciprocity because its behavior seems so closed and controlling. Still, Apple is using—even if reluctantly—a give-to-grow logic.

We think that it is fine for Apple to charge for the software development kit, since charging for it requires people to engage seriously. Free is not necessarily better in this case, since it doesn't require commitment. Being free is not required for reciprocity advantage as long as something is given and something is gained for more players. Apple gives access and through this access has seeded millions of small businesses with the App Store.

The introduction of the iPhone in 2005 forever changed the digital appliance landscape, including mobile phones and mobile computing. Sales of iPhones have been spectacular, but the spread of apps has been much more surprising. The App Store represents both an enormous reciprocity advantage for Apple and a creation engine for small businesses.

The story behind Apple's App Store is similar to Microsoft Kinect in that Apple—Steve Jobs, in particular—did not want third-party apps at first, since Apple feared they would violate the internal elegance of the Apple operating system.[24] Apple was perhaps an even earlier example of involuntary scalable reciprocity than was Microsoft Kinect. Apple was more or less forced to practice reciprocity but came to see the dramatic advantages.

We recognize some will see irony in including Apple as an example of reciprocity advantage, but it also makes the point that you don't have to like the way a company does business in order to benefit from it. Though many find their practices distasteful, Apple still has a reciprocity advantage that benefits others as well as themselves. The many successful app businesses on the iPhone platform are possible only because of the access to the huge number of iPhone users that Apple is willing to share—for a price.

The iPhone is the platform that made a new reciprocity advantage possible. All around the world, entrepreneurs have started small businesses by writing apps and posting them to the App Store. Apple gives away access but charges for the software developer kit and pockets a large percentage of all App Store sales. However unpopular this action might be, the iPhone right-of-way is so valuable that Apple can command the fees. It's merely executing the option to take a piece of the business it helped create.

APPLE'S RECIPROCITY ADVANTAGE IN SUMMARY

What right-of-way does Apple share with others? Apple gives access to the iPhone user base through the App Store marketplace.

Who are Apple's partners in the App Store?

- Individuals who want to develop mobile businesses.
- Companies who want to disrupt entrenched competitors.

How did Apple experiment to learn? Not originally part of the iPhone introduction, internal developers and the outside world saw the need for the Software Developer Kit (SDK) to allow third-party developers to create new apps for the iPhone. After nine months of experimenting with a variety of apps, Steve Jobs agreed to make the SDK and create an open app store as part of the iPhone launch.

What assets does Apple give away? The Software Development Kit, which allows developers access to iPhone users and credit card links to iTunes accounts for billing.

How did the Apple App Store scale? Apple created the Software Development Kit to allow anyone to develop an app, and then it let the apps grow, using the huge base of iPhones for immediate global distribution.

What is Apple's reciprocity advantage? The App Store that offers opportunity to create a new business on a global platform. "There's an app for that."

So What?

By 2012 there were almost 1 million apps and more than 50 billion downloads. In 2013, Apple sold $10 billion in apps, netting $3 billion for Apple and creating an estimated $70 billion collection of new businesses.[25] Whimsical games like Angry Birds revolutionized gaming, for example, while Uber is changing taxis by offering rides at the touch of your iPhone. There is now a pressure on every company to have an app for their business. Google followed. Then with the iPad, mobile devices became a dominant platform for business. Apple now estimates that nearly 300,000 jobs have been created by the "app economy."[26] Some corporations are so concerned that apps might disrupt their existing business that a new slang is emerging in the form of this question: can your business be apped?

Like Apple, Amazon is a secretive company that has embraced huge scaled partnering in order to create growth. Amazon has completely disrupted the publishing business, starting with reinventing bookstores and more recently with the Kindle and ebooks. Their ebook platform makes it easy for anyone to publish a book, but you do have to play by their rules, just like you do if you use Apple's App Store. And of course, you have to pay Amazon.

A still more daring example of sharing right-of-way comes from how Amazon has embraced its competitors by selling goods on the Amazon website. Right alongside Amazon's own offering of anything you want to purchase will be additional offerings from Amazon's partners (also called competitors). These partners typically undercut Amazon's price or sell lower-cost, used alternatives. Why would any retailer do this? It certainly doesn't happen in traditional stores. Untapped revenue is the answer. Amazon currently derives 40 percent of its total sales from partners in their "Associates" program.[27] Nearly half of Amazon's sales come from sharing its right-of-way with direct competitors! A question to consider: might you be missing out on half of your sales?

A reciprocity advantage happens only when people learn new ways to make money through practicing reciprocity. It's not a reciprocity advantage until you scale it. Once you find your reciprocity advantage, you must let it propagate as fast as it can. Competitive advantage is often fleeting. Reciprocity advantages can be enduring.

The good news is that propagation will become much easier. New York University professor Clay Shirky was just a bit ahead of the curve when he wrote in *Here Comes Everybody*:

> This linking together in turn lets us tap our cognitive surplus, the trillion hours a year of free time the educated population of the planet has to spend doing things they care about. In the 20th century, the bulk of that time was spent watching television, but our cognitive surplus is so enormous that diverting even a tiny fraction of time from consumption to participation can create enormous positive effects.[28]

Now momentum is growing, and what Shirky foresaw is ramping up rapidly. Gameful engagement is a great way to amplify scale through what Clay calls the "cognitive surplus." The cognitive surplus is an incredible resource for experimenting to learn, but even more important, it is an incredible resource for scaling once you create your reciprocity advantage.

Shirky's subtitle *The Power of Organizing without Organizations* was and *is* provocative, but what is happening is that new organizational forms are stretching the old organizations—though usually not replacing them. The only traditional organizations that are disappearing are those that don't get this shift. The App Store has made possible a new kind of organizing that is fueling small business growth—as well as Apple profits.

Strategies for Scaling Reciprocity

So far in this book, we've explored the reciprocity advantages of TED, IBM, Microsoft Kinect, the Global Food Safety Initiative, Google Fiber, TechShop, Amazon, and Apple's App Store.

The best names for a product or service are extremely clear and compelling—such as *Smarter Planet*. When it comes time to scale, you want to grow as rapidly as possible. If you get the naming right, it draws you toward the future. If your name is wrong or fuzzy, you fight with it all the way—as do your customers. Your name should be very clear about what you are doing but very flexible about how you will get there. In order to scale rapidly, the name should embody a compelling story.

IBM's Smarter Planet is a purpose-driving strategy that is easy to tell as a compelling story. Smarter Planet is a higher calling within which all of IBM's business activities are now framed. To measure the impact of the initiative, IBM developed a new metric beyond the traditional return on investment (ROI). Called "Expanded Value for Smarter Planet," it evaluates not only operational improvements but also related positive impacts on the world outside IBM. The Smarter Planet is now central to IBM's strategy. IBM employees find the initiative very motivating, especially when compared to the company's old Big Blue baggage. Compelling stories lead to more engaged employees, partners, and customers.

The name *Smarter Planet* is meaningful, motivational, and intuitive. There is a simple lesson here: if you have a bold vision for your right-of-way, think hard about what you call it. Seek clarity and aspiration. Avoid acronyms, unless you stumble on one that actually does motivate people and express the image of the future you are seeking.

Notice how the words to describe a reciprocity advantage can trumpet their story:

"Ideas worth spreading" (TED)
"Food safety should not be a competitive advantage." (GFSI)

Stories have always been important to grow brands, and they will continue to be important. Kendall Haven is a master storyteller who is also working on the Narrative Networks program launched by the Defense Advanced Research Projects Agency. Haven's book *Story Proof* presents scientific proof that "story structure" is an information delivery system that is evolutionarily hardwired into human brains.[29] This research provides data to demonstrate how our brains are wired to look for stories. If our brains don't find stories, they make them up.

When we hear a great story, our brains are stimulated by dopamine and oxytocin, for example, so that we literally and measurably feel better. This understanding of the value of storytelling opens new opportunities for organizations to apply storytelling in precise ways to make information understandable and engaging.

Neuroscience is yielding data to document the value of storytelling, plus practical guidelines for telling stories that are most convincing. Scaling will happen much faster if it rides on a great story.

New Tools and Practices for Scaling

The future tools for propagation and scaling will become much more lightweight and practical, in several senses. The digital technologies that enable scaling are literally lighter than the massive industrial technologies that they are replacing. Beyond this, organizations themselves have become more lightweight because now a few people can produce economic value that in previous years would have taken an organization of hundreds to manage—as we have seen through the App Store. More partners can be involved with less formal organization.

Perhaps the most dramatic example of this shift is 3D printing. Imagine going to a website to browse an online catalog. You look through the selection and choose a toy that looks like the perfect present for a child's upcoming birthday. At the end of the transaction, however, you do not select the "ship" option. Instead, you hit a button that says "print" and watch as the gift is mechanically fabricated before your eyes. Increasingly, design and distribution can live in the cloud, with local manufacturing in the form of 3D printing. For some products, this will be a game changer. Rather than building large manufacturing infrastructure and then transporting the goods, the design would remain central while the production would be local—if local infrastructure for 3D printing is available in local centers or even in the home.

This kind of desktop manufacturing has been a dream of technologists for a generation. Now, the nascent potential of 3D printing is beginning to crystallize into everyday reality. Finally, in the last few years, a number of consumer-priced 3D printers have made it to the market. The most emblematic was the MakerBot, a home 3D printer invented by maker movement maven Bre Pettis. The original MakerBot came unassembled in a kit that users put together at home. Like all 3D printers, the MakerBot builds objects one layer at a time, precisely "printing" one level of material (usually plastic) on top of another until the object is completed.

Consider this personal maker story: Karl's son Alan was a student at Carnegie Mellon University. Christmas was approaching, and Karl and his wife Elizabeth—being practical parents—asked Alan what he'd like. He said that the one thing he really thought was cool was this new 3D printer, the MakerBot.

It wasn't hard to convince Karl, since he'd wanted to try out the MakerBot too. He had heard about the idea of personal fabricators from Neil Gershenfeld at MIT's Media Lab in the late 1990s. But now the future was becoming practical. So they bought a MakerBot for Alan and played with it together over his winter break.

After assembling the kit, Alan pulled down and modified some practice objects from the "Thingverse," the commons of designs available from other MakerBot owners on the web. Next, Alan needed a project.

So Karl and Elizabeth had a suggestion for him. A small hinge on a cabinet door had broken and couldn't be repaired or replaced. They had tried not using that door, but now they had an alternative. In a matter of hours Alan had created a 3D model of the hinge, printed a plastic version, modified the design, printed more prototypes, and made a replacement hinge that worked.

But plastic is not a good solution for a furniture hinge. So Alan sent the file electronically from Palo Alto to the 3D printing company Shapeways in London, where the hinge was made out of metal and finished in antique brass. Two weeks later they had a replacement hinge.

The future of spare parts businesses will never be the same.

3D printing will disrupt Home Depot, Lowes, and parts stores of all kinds. And you won't need the skills to make a hinge or many replacement parts because there will be a place to go where you can get it done and it will feel a lot like TechShop does today.

While the technology is in its early stages, the potential for streamlining the scaling process is staggering. Designers, for example, will be able to produce and make necessary changes to a physical prototype in a matter of hours, not weeks. At present, 3D printing is best suited to tinkering with the physical forms of objects, but more complex functions are on the horizon. Indeed, applications of the technology in many fields are well under way: in medicine, tissue will be printed from stem cells; in electronics, basic circuits and components can be printed; and in construction, masonry walls and structures can be printed. On the other hand, 3D printing of real guns is now possible. 3D printing will be amazing, but what gets printed will be up to the people doing the printing.

While 3D printing is emblematic of the emerging capabilities of distributed innovation and scaling, the field's roots extend deep into the technology of the Internet itself. Indeed, in many ways, distributed production can be thought of as the extension of peer-to-peer network principles to manufacturing processes.

3D printing will accelerate the move to mass customization and scaling, where production is done on a large scale, and yet products have a personal or customized feel. At the level of individual shoppers, distributed innovation will allow insights and innovations that are developed in a particular context or region not only to be quickly transmitted to other locations, but also quickly modified and adapted to specific circumstances. Rapid recombination will be the rule. At an individual level, this translates into yet more energy behind attempts at mass customization and particularly behind those practices that give people a greater human connection to the products and services that they use. It is interesting to note that visionary Stan Davis, in his landmark book *Future Perfect*, first introduced the concept of mass customization in 1987. Now, finally, mass customization will become possible on a large scale, and it will accelerate the process of scaling in ways that we can only begin to imagine today.

At the beginning of the computer revolution, individual desktop machines were the workhorses of both businesses and home users. Over time, however, with the emergence of the Internet, online software and services have become increasingly important. Indeed, we are now at an inversion point. As centralized systems enter their twilight, and mobile platforms reach their zenith, the cloud is the place to look for future innovations in computation. The cloud will be the amplifier for propagation—not just innovation.

Over the next decade, new cloud-based services will become available, not only in the developed world, but in the developing world as well. There is strong evidence that cloud-connected smart phones are on track to follow the same trajectory that cell phones have, as they became widespread across the developing world and see dramatic price decreases over time. The cloud will be inherently and enthusiastically global.

All of this, of course, could be very disruptive to established players who fail to adapt to this new dynamic. There are possibilities for hyper-competition to emerge in cloud-served environments, as many of the original ideas about a friction-free online marketplace that accompanied early dot-com thinkers are brought closer to reality—at least for digital goods. Look for new monetization models to emerge and for mix-and-match approaches to be empowered as the cloud allows for extensive experimentation and substitutions. Within the cloud individual services can be seen as analogous to fluid utilities or data flows. Adjusting and balancing these flows is an art that will be increasingly appreciated.

Shoppers, too, will have the power of supercomputing driving their purchasing decisions. They will have access to as much or as little information as they desire, and neither manufacturers nor retailers will be able to control the flow of this information, even in the buying environment. However, they could offer trusted filtering options. Indeed, competition for trusted filters at the point of purchase will be fierce. Trust will fuel scale.

Reciprocity will be increasingly scalable.

Future Forces That Will Demand Reciprocity

————

The future that you anticipated has been cancelled.

ORCHESTRAL MANOEUVRES IN THE DARK,
English Electric (2013)

————

The future forces of the next decade will disrupt traditional transactional models for doing business. These same future forces will call for reciprocity as an important way to promote business growth on a very large scale.

In Part Two, we discuss four future forces that we believe will shape and disrupt your ability to uncover your right-of-way, to find the best partners, to develop a give-to-learn strategy, and to scale your business for greater impact. This introduction provides a broad futures context for the four future forces we think will be most important to consider.

The Institute for the Future has been creating ten-year forecasts since 1968. IFTF sometimes jokingly observes that it may be the only futures group ever to outlive its own forecasts. Even though nobody can predict the future, IFTF forecasts are designed to provoke your insight—to help you make your own future and become more resilient. Over its history of more than 40 years, 60–80 percent of the futures that IFTF has forecasted have actually happened. The ten-year forecast that we are sharing in this book is both hopeful and frightening.

Even in a VUCA World, almost nothing is truly new. To quote cyberpunk novelist William Gibson, "The future is already here— it's just not evenly distributed."[30] We look for those signals of the future and use them to bring our forecasts to life. We then share that foresight to provoke insight and action. People take action based on their own insights—even if they don't agree with our forecasts. Our goal is not to predict the future but to provoke insights and better decisions in the present.

We are already living in a world of uncomfortable Ands—such as extreme abundance and biting scarcity, widespread obesity and rampant hunger, hyper-connectivity and gnawing isolation. We are entering a world of increasing Ands, though most people don't realize it yet. Reciprocity advantage will make a lot more business sense in a world of And. Reciprocity will rise in the context of a VUCA World, with signals all around us as it comes to life.

These are the disruptions that we feel will demand reciprocity. Reciprocity can bring out the hope in these forces and overcome the fear.

Chapter 5. The digital natives—eighteen years old or younger in 2014—will create new rights-of-way and new practices for engagement. They will have greater connection and greater global empathy. The media ecology around these young people as they become adults is unlike any other with global social media, vivid gaming interfaces, and supercomputing resources available in some form for a rapidly increasing proportion of the global population.

Chapter 6. Socialstructing will create new ways to partner and work together across great distances. Traditional jobs will be reimagined through a reciprocity lens as ways of working together across great distances becomes much easier and cost effective. This will be a world with fewer traditional jobs and lower job security, but more flexibility and ways to make a living. In the next ten years, intellectual property will shift from more closed to more open, but it will be a very messy process along the way.

Chapter 7. Gameful engagement will disrupt how we learn and how we experiment. Gameful engagement is emotionally laden attention. As the digital natives become adults, they will force traditional marketing, advertising, and commercials to be reimagined as gameful engagement.

Chapter 8. Cloud-served supercomputing will become the world's largest amplifier, and its currency will be reciprocity. The network will become the computer, with profound implications. The online and in-person worlds will be increasingly blended.

All four of these future forces will be laced with both hope and threat—again, a world of And, not *Or.* Reciprocity will be countered by exploitation in a wild new mix of possibilities that will be laced with good and evil. Reciprocity can go wrong. There will be ugly aspects of scalable reciprocity, though we believe that the overall direction will be for greater good.

These external future forces will be unpredictable, but the directions of change are clear. These future forces cannot be controlled, but they can be influenced and shaped. These four forces are giant waves of change. If you cannot ride the waves, you can at least avoid being hit by them. These forces will all demand reciprocity, each in different ways.

Part Two of this book puts the search for reciprocity advantage in a futures context—jumping out ten years and looking back. What are the external future forces of the next decade that will shape the four steps to scalable reciprocity—either by slowing progress or accelerating it?

We have learned in our custom forecasting for CEOs and top executives that it is important to boil every custom forecast down to four or five external future forces that all the top leaders should consider as filters for everyday decisions.

Bob had a dramatic experience of this need for clarity in his first meeting with the new CEO of a Fortune 100 company. The new CTO also attended the meeting and reported that on his first day on the job, he had received 23 different "trend reports"—none coordinated and all using different language to describe similar concepts. The CEO turned to Bob and said, "Can't you do better than that? Can't you get it down to three or at the most five future forces that all the top leaders should consider?"

That was indeed a difficult challenge, but we have come to realize that the CEO was exactly right. A forecast needs to have great clarity; it needs to be simple—but not simplistic. At Institute for the Future, we now call this honing process *Forecaster's Haiku*. While we were writing this book, our IFTF colleague Miriam Lueck Avery shared an example of someone literally using haiku in a forecast. Oceanographer Greg Johnson used haiku to summarize the Intergovernmental Panel on Climate Change (IPCC) report.[31] We found this effort at blending science and poetry inspiring. You'll see our humble efforts at haiku forecasts at the front of each chapter in Part Two.

Part Two draws from IFTF's latest foundational forecasts in search of those that will shape reciprocity advantage. These four future forces will be part of a VUCA World that will be increasingly disrupted.[32] It is likely to get even worse than the VUCA Worlds we have experienced in the past. Still, there is great hope.

A VUCA World on Steroids

We are entering what we think will be the most turbulent decade in any of our lifetimes—*and* the most hopeful. Social unrest will abound, unless the rich-poor gap gets smaller—which currently seems unlikely. Mobility will be a gnawing issue if poor people have little hope of ever improving their lot. Meanwhile, calls for social justice are resonating globally. We live in an increasingly jagged economy, with many sharp edges.

By thinking ten years ahead, it is possible for one to look through the VUCA fog to reveal how growth and scale might be achieved. By looking at and listening for the future, you learn that

- **Volatility** will call out for **Vision.** (What is your vision for growth and scale?) Scalable reciprocity is a visionary opportunity that is just becoming practical. In some cases, scalable reciprocity will become mandatory.

- **Uncertainty** will call out for **Understanding.** (What do you need to understand more deeply in order to achieve growth and scale?) Scalable reciprocity is based on a different understanding of business in the context of the disruptive future forces all around us.

- **Complexity** will call out for **Clarity.** (In order to win in the VUCA World, leaders must be very clear about where they want to go but very flexible in how they get there.) Scalable reciprocity requires clarity of direction combined with the ability to respond on the fly.

- **Ambiguity** will call out for **Agility.** (To achieve growth and scale, leaders must be fit—physically and mentally.) Scalable reciprocity is more rewarding than win/lose transactional forms of business, but it requires leaders to engage gracefully in urgent situations.

One of the biggest challenges in creating new businesses is designing for a changing world. Part Two explains how the world will be different, so you can build these differences into your plans. The four future forces that we introduce will disrupt old economic models and create opportunities for new ones.

CHAPTER 5

How the Digital Natives Will Disrupt Rights-of-Way

Kids seeing spaces
for mutual benefit
New models for trust

———

To pay continuous partial attention is to pay partial
attention—CONTINUOUSLY. It is motivated by a desire
to be a LIVE node on the network ... To be busy, to be
connected, is to be alive, to be recognized, and to matter.

LINDA STONE,
"Continuous Partial Attention"

———

Linda Stone has done more than anyone to explore how we digital immigrants can begin to understand digital natives. In ten years, everyone on the planet 28 years old or younger—rich or poor—will be a digital native. We call them digital natives because they grew up in the interconnected world of early-stage social media, vivid video gaming interfaces, and early-stage cloud-served supercomputing.

The media ecology of TV shaped the Baby Boomers as they became adults. Today's Millennials, or Generation Y, are often thought of as digital natives, but they are too old for that. In 2014, the digital natives are 18 or younger; and the younger they are, the more new digital media will shape this group of leaders who will make the future.

The real digital natives will demand new rights-of-way in physical and virtual space. They also will speak or text or videotape their own languages, tell their own stories, and embody a wild mix of cultures—all amplified through the cloud on a global scale.

Demography Is a Trend, but the Digital Natives Will Be a Disruption

Demography is a tool that can predict the future, in a way—at least at the level of macro trends. Compared to shifts in technology, the metrics of birthrates and lifespans are slower to change, and some of their likely impact can be seen decades in advance. Take the needs of America's Baby Boom generation, for example. It is clear that widespread demographic awareness has fueled massive innovation, as enterprising entrepreneurs have rushed to create products and services for this unusually large cohort, all the way from cradle to impending retirement.

Yet, while demographics can be rocket fuel for product innovation, it is becoming clear that demographic trends can have unpredictable implications as well. Indeed, diverging demographic trends are beginning to solidify around what are likely to be some of the fundamental cultural fault lines of the next century. In addition, although macro-level demographics generally supply predictable outcomes, these divergent demographics do not.

The gap between rich and poor is already stark and visible from both sides—and it is widening. To make things worse, it is very difficult to move from poverty into an improved economic situation. Having people stuck in poverty is both inexcusable and dangerous. Having large numbers of digital natives stuck in poverty will be explosive. This gap will be a major disruptive force as the digital natives become adults—especially if upward mobility continues to be so challenging. But demographic tensions run deeper still at both the individual and the global level and will ultimately result in deep schisms.

The digital natives will disrupt rights-of-way over the next decade in ways that we can only begin to imagine. Most kids become adults physically between the ages of 13 and 15, depending on the kid and the culture. The process of maturing, however, occurs at different rates and is influenced more or less by the media. Whatever media ecology they grow up with will shape the rest of their lives—whether we realize it or not.

Today's kids have thousands of TV channels, ubiquitous social media, and incredibly vivid video gaming interfaces—a media ecology unlike any other in history. So the digital natives are leading digital immigrants into uncharted territory. In ten years, for example, sensors will be everywhere, they will be very cheap, many of them will be connected, and some of them will be in our bodies. The potential for vivid interactive interfaces will increase dramatically.

Tomorrow's adults will have grown up with digital interfaces for television, social media, gaming—and pretty much all facets of life—that are much more immersive and engaging than anything adults have in offices today. Just think about the user interface that the best of today's video games offer, independent of content. Vivid user interfaces will make digital tools much more accessible and compelling. Right now, video gaming interfaces are dramatically better than anything most users experience in offices. These ways in which young people interact with digital media—and interact with each other—will continue to expand dramatically. The digital natives understand their own media very well but know little about current data-processing environments, for example. By the time this generation hits the office workforce, systems will resemble the media that they bring to work with them. Even today in many parts of the world, Millennials find that the digital tools they use at work are far behind the tools they use in their personal lives. For many young people, going to the office means downgrading their digital media resources.

It is the quality of the *interface* currently available in video games that is so great and so rich—not—in most cases—the content. Over the next decade, interfaces will become even better.

Kids becoming adults in the next ten years will have a sense that they can connect personally with anyone on the planet—and they will be correct. This sense of global connectedness could spawn a new era of global empathy, although it is too early to tell. What is apparent is that growing up in a digitally enhanced world will be different—*very* different—for better *and* for worse.

Will the Digital Natives Be Truly Different?

If so, *how* different? We think they will, but we must admit that one of the biggest traps in ten-year forecasting is to confuse what you want to happen with what you think will happen. We are very optimistic about the digital natives and think they will have greater global empathy. Still, there are troubling youth behaviors, such as cyber bullying. Whatever paths they choose, it is the digital natives who will most disrupt rights-of-way and networks of trust, stretching all of us in unfathomable ways.

Babies in 2014 are tapping their first screen and learning to slide their fingers across that screen almost from birth. Just *how* new media will affect the way they think is still unknown, but it will certainly be profound.

If you are lucky enough to have a child who is a digital native, you have a wonderful opportunity for reverse mentoring—your own experience of gameful engagement can be enhanced if you play with a digital native. But even if you aren't the parent of a digital native, you can reach out and find digital natives from whom you can learn. Fortunately, we elders still have perspectives and experience to offer—even though the digital natives have neurocapabilities and skills that digital immigrants will never have. Cross-generational mentoring is the most important single strategy we know for learning about the future and navigating the next decade.

Digital technology is transforming into digitally enhanced life. We used to think of either shopping in a store or shopping online. Now, even when shopping in a store, people use their smart phones to gather information on pricing and product performance online. Discreet channels of commerce are blending into omni-channel shopping.

Filters will be everywhere as we move from the Internet as we know it today to tomorrow's cloud-served supercomputing. The smart phones of 2014 will look crude in comparison to what will be available in 2024 as the interfaces become more graceful and transparent. Everyone will have some filters. The choices will be *which* filters and who will curate the content that will be filtered. Even the perceptions of rights-of-way will be filtered. Filters will give corporations permission to play in certain spaces but will also discourage them from playing in others.

Some filters will allow us to be more open, to reach out in ways we have never reached out before. Some filters will be more closed, so they protect us from things we don't want to hear or see. Extreme filters could even allow people to hear only opinions with which they already agree.

Digital immigrants are offline, unless we choose to go online.

Digital natives will always be online, unless they choose to disconnect. They will view life through a digital overlay. This virtual overlay could help them learn, for instance, what species of tree they are looking up at in a forest.

Education will take on a new meaning in this emerging world. Education innovator Milton Chen, for example, talks about "Ed-YOU-cation," which focuses on individual learning, rather than transferring a particular body of knowledge. He studies people he calls "extreme learners," who are stretching the limits of today's schools.[33]

Personal virtual overlays will be able to help digital natives make all kinds of choices—drawing from their own networks of trust. For example, an overlay could distinguish which products to purchase based on a person's values. An overlay could open users to new ideas or it could protect them from any ideas that don't align with their beliefs. The digitally enhanced world will present tomorrow's adults with more options than ever to either engage or detach.

If anything, this increasing generational and demographic fragmentation points to the need for new common languages and ways to somehow bridge these divides.

For those who are 30 years old or younger, a generation is only about six years—and shrinking. Certainly, most 30-year-olds are adept with the current forms of social media. However, they are two generations out of touch with the true digital natives.

Those young people in the rough age range of 18 to 30 are in an awkward gap in terms of generations. They may think they are digital natives, but they are not. Many are having trouble finding first jobs. Many have needed to move back in with their parents. Many, unfortunately, will find that true digital natives will get the jobs that they wish they had. In 2006, Anya Kamanetz wrote a book about this cohort called *Generation Debt* with the disturbing subtitle *Why Now Is a Terrible Time to Be Young.*[34] Our forecast is that the true digital natives will fare much better across their age cohort than those who are just a bit older.

Even though the majority of the age cohort between 17 and 30 is struggling to land first jobs and pay off debt, some of the most successful Silicon Valley entrepreneurs are also in this group. Again, this is a world of And. The most successful red-hot innovators are creating companies that service the needs that they see and experience. In his article on money and politics in Silicon Valley, *New Yorker* reporter George Packer writes: "It suddenly occurred to me that the hottest tech start-ups are solving all the problems of being twenty years old, with cash on hand, because that's who thinks them up."[35]

The next generation rights-of-way, expressed in next-gen language, will come from the digital natives. Language expresses and communicates right-of-way. Stories bring together those languages and spread the word.

Language Will Change as the Digital Natives Become Adults

As we think ten years ahead about reciprocity advantage, consider the importance of language and how the digital natives write, think, and communicate. Careful framing of the future with just the right words will be very important to reach them. If you use the right words and concepts, digital natives will draw you toward the kind future you want to create. If you don't use the right words, your failure to communicate will constrain you. For example, instead of calling them consumers, the best companies are already calling them what they should have been called all along: people.

IFTF has done custom forecasting in support of United Cerebral Palsy and the community of organizations who work with people with disabilities. In this world, the People First Principle prevails. Rather than saying someone is "disabled" or "handicapped" or "a diabetic," the People First Principle suggests that you always lead with the word *people* or *person*, for example, a *person with disabilities*, a *person with diabetes*, or *people with disabilities*.

It is time for the rest of us—especially marketers and advertisers—to adopt the People First Principle. The future will demand big changes, so why not start now and get ahead of them, or at least catch up?

Framing a conversation about right-of-way in the future must go much further than the unfortunate word *consumer*. We discussed in Chapter One how right-of-way in the world of business is mostly about spans of trust and networks of trust—not legal sanctions. Trust is often embedded in words that have special meaning for particular communities. Language frames rights-of-way. In today's marketplace, building trust is the responsibility of marketing and advertising organizations that do brand building.

In the next ten years, the term *marketing* will be disrupted, as will *advertising* and *commercials*, as trust and trust building transform in the blended-reality world of cloud-served supercomputing, as we will discuss in much more detail in Chapter 8. Certainly, marketing has been instrumental in the introduction of new products and broadening their use—as is clear with the mobile phone market.

Rights-of-way will be uncovered, cultivated, nurtured, and grown through cloud-amplified networks of trust. Instead of calling it *marketing*, *advertising*, or *commercials*, the best companies are already calling it what they should have been calling it all along: engagement.

The digital natives will distrust traditional marketing and not want to be marketed to; they will want to be engaged with. The younger you are, the more you already expect this kind of engagement. The digital natives will demand it in the future, so why not start now?

Corporations must uncover their own rights-of-way, the spaces where they are trusted and have permission to innovate with the digital natives. They cannot claim new rights-of-way, unless they are authentic and perceived as within the span of trust for that particular company. You cannot advertise to create right-of-way that isn't there already. Corporations must engage with their network of trust to grow it through authentic trust building and actions that will ease into rights-of-way. Growing your right-of-way will be increasingly about nurturing and amplifying you own networks of trust. If you can grow your span of trust, you can widen your reciprocity right-of-way.

Digital Natives, Digital Leapfrogs

The term *digital divide* now seems almost quaint. It used to be true that rich kids had access to digital technology, but poor kids did not. Now, almost everyone has access to some connective technology. In ten years, it is reasonable to believe that everyone on the planet—even those who are poor, hungry, and hopeless—will have access to significant connectivity.

The world has always had a rich-poor gap, and it continues to grow in both emerging and developed economies. At Institute for the Future, we have reviewed the rich-poor gap over time and done a range of forecasts, and the situation is unlikely to get better. What's really new is not the gap itself but its *visibility*. Poor people will be able to see the very wealthy much more clearly, perhaps even in high definition. If poor digital natives don't have realistic hopes that they can improve their lives, they will be extremely frustrated. It is one thing to be hungry and hopeless, but it is quite another to be hungry, hopeless, and connected.

Digital natives in emerging markets will have the potential to leap-frog developed worlds without following the same slow evolutionary paths. Perhaps the best example of leapfrogging in action is the mobile phone. Essentially, this device simply bypassed altogether the whole massive problem of the "last mile," which had bedeviled the telecommunications networks of more technologically advanced nations for several decades. The "last mile" was the distance from the last network node to the home of the telephone user. Mobile telephony just skipped through the air over that last mile. It was as if, by embracing mobile telephony, these emerging economies skipped over a lifetime of incremental improvements in telecommunications to join the most technologically advanced nations on earth as peers, unencumbered by ingrained habits, and all straight out of the starting gate.

Leapfrog innovations, however, are often jagged: sharply up in some areas, sharply down in others—with many cutting edges. Some very small players will become lead innovators on a global stage through the cloud. In fact, partnerships between very large and very small players will become much more common over the next decade. Virtual and physical worlds will blur—online and in-store shopping will blend, for example. Leapfrogging will create new rights-of-way, new ways to imagine how innovation might occur. Rights-of-way will still need to be uncovered, but once uncovered, it will become possible to amplify them quite rapidly.

By 2024, everyone on the planet 28 or younger—rich or poor—will be a digital native. This age cohort will drive innovation styles and practices in all aspects of life, including commercial and political. Indeed, the unrest across North Africa and the Middle East in 2011 only hinted at the future disruptions that are not just possible, but probable—unless the rich-poor gap somehow narrows.

These global digital natives will see rights-of-way very differently. For example, Michael Conroy has written a book called *Branded! How the "Certification Revolution" Is Transforming Corporations.*[36] Conroy argues that NGOs (nongovernmental organizations) are creating new means of certification that rate brands by independent criteria based on explicit values and interests. NGO certification is a particular kind of right-of-way, somewhere between what is legal and what is trusted. Imagine such certification coming from digital natives from anywhere in the world with any particular kind of concern. Digital natives will be able to shape how rights-of-way are perceived and then amplify their concerns very effectively through online media. A company may label itself "green" and may in fact actually be green, but what if an NGO rates them as otherwise—fairly or unfairly? The digital natives will get involved in the certification process with increasing sophistication and are also likely to have strong opinions about which companies have rights-of-way to play where.

Often, it is assumed that regions follow more or less the same developmental trajectory but at different rates, resulting in some areas being a few years behind others. This perspective assumes, however, that emerging regions will follow the same path and use similar technologies as the so-called developed world. The digital natives are a disruption, however, and digital innovations will be introduced directly into developing regions without first installing legacy infrastructure that was required elsewhere in earlier times. Such leapfrogging will be very disruptive and will reveal new rights-of-way.

Who has rights-of-way around this kind of innovation? It could be the mobile carriers, but it could also be companies that are engaged in particular businesses that make use of the new mobile infrastructure. When infrastructures of trust overlap with infrastructures of connectivity, new rights-of-way will emerge.

For example, large manufacturers interested in reaching people in developing markets can start by linking with local kiosk operators, who can order and learn through the new mobile networks. In this case, the right-of-way could be retailing expertise, delivered through mobile networks. P&G, Nestlé, and Unilever all have programs that are seeking to nurture these rights-of-way and grow their businesses in local markets by supporting local retailers (often individuals operating small stands or kiosks), who then agree to carry and sell their products. By supporting these very small businesses, large manufacturers can also sell more of their own products through new retail channels in new markets. These companies are nurturing new rights-of-way.

The Digital Natives Will Be Attracted by IP-Free Practices

In ten years, digital native entrepreneurs, aggressive small businesses, and hackers will be everywhere, and most of them will be globally connected. These groups will always be searching for new ideas, and they will feed on, cooperate with, and compete with each other. Current crowdfunding efforts, such as Kickstarter and Indiegogo, signal a new era of constant experimentation and rapid growth of both new ideas and new companies. The digital natives will drive increasing use of crowdfunding. The digital natives are also not nearly as abiding of closed intellectual property as were their parents—or even their older brothers and sisters. Your existing—even if unrealized—right-of-way will be fair game for these hungry innovators.

Thus, there is a defensive reason to uncover your right-of-way—so that you can protect it from others. The worst scenario would be if someone else were to uncover and develop your right-of-way and you had to buy it back at an exorbitant price. Better to uncover your right-of-way yourself.

Here is a question for every business leader to ponder: how might a digital native introduce a new business in my right-of-way?

In these days of rapid prototyping and ubiquitous startups, lots of people will be sniffing around your right-of-way without you even knowing it. Right-of-way will be at the root of reciprocity advantage, but it may also mean survival for some companies.

What will right-of-way mean in a world where it is becoming increasingly difficult to own intellectual property (IP)? The space where you are trusted may well be a space you cannot own. In fact, in some parts of the world already, it is becoming impossible to own intellectual property. The digital natives clearly have a very different view of intellectual property than their elders.

The direction for intellectual property over the next ten years will go from closed to more open, but it will be a very messy process along the way. In many cases, it will be much more attractive to think of

IP as currency that must be exchanged to derive value, rather than property that must be protected. The most viable business strategy in the future, as digital natives become adults, is more likely to resemble TED's rights management than Sony's.

Even as battles over intellectual property rage, much of the world is already patent-free because companies are choosing not to spend the money necessary to secure patents that may not be enforced anyway. Rather, these companies are exploring new ways to engage with others to *expand* the impact of intellectual property, not just protect it. In Silicon Valley, IP lawyers used to focus exclusively on protecting each new product—even each new idea—whenever possible. Companies wanted to own IP, to own ideas. Now, when new products are nearing the marketplace, lawyers ask a question that had rarely been asked before: what if we gave this away in a creative way? How might we make even more money giving it away strategically, rather than fighting to protect it? This idea will become even more attractive when it becomes impossible to protect the new idea anyway.

The digital natives—in many different ways and from many different places—will disrupt and reimagine rights-of-way. Very few corporations or even universities are prepared for the digital natives.

Where it is possible to own IP, it makes sense for companies to try to enforce it. Protecting IP, however, will become much harder over the next decade. In many cases, it will be smarter to uncover your right-of-way and give away small amounts of access to these assets in order to learn how to make money in new ways. This is the essence of the reciprocity advantage and why it will be the wave of the future in a world led by digital natives.

CHAPTER 6

How Socialstructing Will Disrupt Partnering

Partners everywhere
more ways to make a living
fewer jobs of worth

———

It's amazing what people are now able to do with no money, no
management, and no employees.... Shaped by technologies we
are only just beginning to deploy, the very underpinnings of our
society and institutions—from how we work to how we create
value, govern, trade, learn, and innovate—are being reshaped.

MARINA GORBIS,
The Nature of the Future:
Dispatches from the Socialstructed World

———

Marina Gorbis was born in Russia during the days of the USSR,
and she escaped as a teenager. She grew up in a social economy gone
amok, but she now sees something quite different emerging that she
calls *socialstructing*, which includes the following:

- Microcontributions
- Nonmonetary rewards
- Technology-enabled sociality
- Community organizers, not managers
- Large network participation

These are the same new tools and new currencies that will disrupt partnering over the next decade. Socialstructing will mean radically new ways of partnering.

Diverse Partnership Possibilities Will Abound

Expect a big shift in the diversity of potential partners—and the diversity of ways in which the partners will be able to work together. In a socialstructed world, partners can come from anywhere, and they can be any size. In particular, we expect more partnerships involving very large and very small players because it will become much easier to find potential partners and work together. Collaboration, teaming, and partnerships will become possible on a scale that could never before have been imagined.

Indeed, the boundaries that determine the size of businesses will become increasingly porous. Traditional corporations have people called *employees* who are doing *jobs*. The bad news is that in ten years, there will be fewer traditional jobs and lower job security. The good news is that in that same time frame, there will be much more flexibility and many more ways to make a living.

The potential for collaboration and new partnerships will explode, even though the models for how these partnerships might work are only beginning to be imagined and prototyped.

Both Hollywood and Silicon Valley have been prototyping this new kind of partnering for years. The Hollywood model of work involves ad hoc commitments to movies while they are under production, but long-term, informal commitments to directors and to social networks of people who work well together. As a new set of partnerships is formed around a new movie, people band together as if they had jobs and as if they worked for a corporation—even though neither is true. Rather, they are committed to working together to finish the film. Once a movie is done, all bets are off, and the Hollywood model starts all over again.

During the early days of Silicon Valley, Bob worked as a research affiliate at MIT and commuted back and forth between Cambridge, Massachusetts, and Silicon Valley. He was amazed at the difference in cultures, and this difference continues. On the east coast, there tends to be a closed culture with lots of secrecy. In Silicon Valley, it is amazing what people are willing to give away in the trust that they will get back even more in return. Drop in on any class or maker meeting, for example, and ideas will be flowing freely. Indeed, Silicon Valley runs on a culture of reciprocity, and that style of collaboration is now spreading.

When Mike Zuckerman had the idea for Freespace, he was building on the tradition and spirit of Silicon Valley but applying it in a new way.[37] Zuckerman convinced a San Francisco landlord to rent him a building for one month for one dollar. He opened a collaborative space for artists, entrepreneurs, craftspeople, and others who wandered in and were willing to play by the two basic rules: "no money, no alcohol." Zuckerman tied Freespace to the National Day of Civic Hacking and seeded a rather large movement. The Freespace San Francisco adventure was extended to six months. Now, similar ventures are being attempted in other parts of the world. Their motto: "A temporary space for lasting change."

Collaboration is the ability to work together for a common purpose. Ad hoc teams, amplified by new media, will allow us ways to work together across great distances. Partnerships imply a great commitment, beyond collaboration and ad hoc teams. Partnerships require that all partners look out for each other—not just for themselves.

The technologies of collaboration will allow partners to extend the boundaries of reciprocity. How wide will you be able to reach out to create new reciprocity-based ventures? The wider your radius of reciprocity, the more agile, robust, and resilient your business model will be in the future. The cloud has the potential to expand your radius of reciprocity globally. New potential partners will appear, and working closely with those new partners will become possible.

Scalable reciprocity will be a way to learn about new markets and allow you to accomplish what you could not do alone. It will lower your innovation risk and increase your impact,. Scalable reciprocity will be a healthy way to live and do business.

More Potential Partners
Means More Ways to Make a Living

Traditionally, corporations and jobs have evolved out of necessity and have been effective ways of organizing work. But it is becoming possible to break tasks down much more precisely than before, and new ways of structuring work are developing rapidly.

For example, oDesk is an international network of companies willing to hire online workers to do specific microtasks. This is not outsourcing jobs. Rather, it is extending the traditional definition of a job by allowing it to be broken down into smaller task units and shared virtually. It is a marketplace and bookkeeper/payroll service for a professional informal economy, in which oDesk handles all the working arrangements. Both workers and employers are rated within the system. Instead of hiring someone to do a job, oDesk makes it possible to hire someone to do a task or a micro task. People from around the world can work flexibly through oDesk, even if they don't have a formal job. Indeed, there are already people making more money through oDesk than they would if they had conventional jobs. Whether or not oDesk succeeds commercially, the infrastructure for global microtask routing is becoming practical. Services like this enable businesses to link with reputable individuals who are seeking work—but not conventional jobs.

Task Rabbit is similar to oDesk, but focused on household tasks. Task Rabbit allows you to contract with individual people who can walk your dog, pick up your groceries, or help with household tasks. One of the most popular microtasks performed via Task Rabbit is assembling IKEA furniture.

This kind of task routing makes new models of partnership possible. Innovation can be broken down into tasks and microtasks. The leadership challenge will be one of coordination and clarity. Leaders in these kinds of socialstructed organizations will have to be very clear where they are going but very flexible about how they get there. All partners will have to be committed. And the terms of engagement will need to be both flexible and robust.

Of course, there is great potential for abuse of workers in a world of global task routing. Already, microunions are forming to protect basic worker rights and decrease the potential for abuse. As work gets broken down into smaller and smaller tasks, it will get harder and harder to control who does what and what they are paid.

Columnist and author Thomas Friedman has argued convincingly that the world is flat and individuals across the entire planet are moving into level competition with one another.[38] By task routing through platforms, such as oDesk, LiveOps, Mobileworks, or Mechanical Turk, it is possible to put people around the entire planet in direct competition with one another—*And* give them the opportunity to cooperate and partner in new ways. It is equally true that the emerging world of work will be both flat and jagged, sharply divided by peaks and valleys of wealth and unrest. This fundamental tension of ideas will cause social tensions, as well as new partnering opportunities. New media will amplify both the hopeful and the threatening sides of the human experience.

New Models for Partnering

The Global Food Safety Initiative (GFSI), introduced in Chapter 2, is an example of partnering to do something that no single company could do alone. Food companies have always been concerned about food safety, and having a good reputation around food safety used to be a competitive advantage. As the food web has become increasingly connected and increasingly global, however, food safety can no longer be a competitive advantage for a single company. A food safety crisis creates consumer concern that disrupts all food providers—even if they have nothing to do with the source of the food scare. Food safety is being reimagined as a foundational standard upon which competition can build. GFSI was started in 2000 as an effort to leverage the resources of corporations, governments, and universities.

Now, through this scalable reciprocity innovation, food safety risk is reduced for both companies and consumers. Competition can occur at a higher level, building on the foundation of great food safety across the industry.

GFSI is an example of how large corporations can accomplish what governments alone cannot. This is especially true for an issue like food safety, which crosses borders and affects so many people. Partners in food safety have to begin on the farm and follow the food through production, processing, distribution, retail, and food service, right up to the people who eat the food.

Through GFSI, companies such as McDonald's, Walmart, Danone, Tesco, Syngenta, and Cargill are giving away their expertise in food safety in the trust that each company will gain larger value in return when food safety becomes less of a concern. Remember that if a food safety issue erupts, any food provider can be affected—even with no involvement whatsoever. So by sharing ways to increase safety, each company is lowering its risk and betting that a safe food environment will give its brand a better chance to compete.

This food safety initiative is moving to the cloud, which will amplify the local and regional efforts to a global scale, potentially allowing for food safety practices to be shared more broadly across more parts of the world more rapidly. The cloud will provide connectivity to avoid food safety breakdowns and also to respond to crises when they occur.

A very different kind of partnering model has been pioneered by Frito-Lay with its Doritos brand. Called Crash the Super Bowl, this effort started seven years ago with a contest that invited anyone to do his or her own Super Bowl commercial. If you won, your commercial would appear in the Super Bowl. These ads score quite well (often better than the professionally produced commercials that cost much more), and the contest gives the company a direct way to engage with the people who use its products. Doritos is partnering with their consumers, not just pushing products through conventional advertising. And they are making it fun. There will be many new ways to expand on partnering with individuals.

Diasporas as Partners

Diaspora is an ancient concept that can be traced back to the Torah—the Jewish diaspora separated from the Promised Land. In today's world, think of a diaspora as a network of trust. Modern diasporas are social networks with shared values that are amplified through the social networks and—increasingly—social media. People have always lived in the context of social networks. In the United States in the late twentieth century, for example, both Hippies and, later, the Yuppies were essentially diasporas based on shared values. Now however, these networks are more varied, more visible, and more electronically connected than in the past. Communities no longer split simply into *mainstream* and *counterculture*, but instead, members identify with several self-defined dimensions. Market segments are dynamic, not static, so one person might be part of a particular market segment for some period but belong to another market segment at a later date.

Partnering with members of diasporas is possible but tricky. Diasporas will amplify commercial innovation, scale, and disruption—*if* their members become committed to a product or service. Companies will need to grow relationships based on trust in order to engage with diasporas. When they are very good and very lucky, companies may even create diasporas of brand loyalty, as Apple or TED have done. Diasporas like to play within rights-of-way, and once they recognize them, innovation increases geometrically. The reason innovation happens faster within diasporas is because of shared values and great trust. Within diasporas, brand trust building happens quickly. Their values are clear and they believe they know who to trust—and who not to trust. If a brand or a company is perceived to be consistent with a diaspora's values, then it will have permission to experiment with new products and services, as long as it stays within the envelope of trust that has been granted.

Diasporas and everyone else will be increasingly able to create their own view of and interface with the world, through cloud-based media tools and filters. Companies increasingly will need to meet people on their terms. When talking to members of a diaspora, there will be a premium on the ability to "speak their language." Within this context, there will be increased emphasis on introductions, guides, curators, filters, and translators.

Not all online social networks are networks of trust or diasporas, however. Social networks are the groups of people with whom individuals choose to personally connect. As people in industrialized regions increasingly put a premium on developing the worldviews that inform their behaviors, it will become commonplace for individuals to share far more of their consumer behaviors with like-minded cohesive subcultures of belief than with their own extended families and even social networks.

Trust will be tracked from person to person, and loss of trust will follow similarly. Transparency will be thrust upon everyone in ways that are not possible today. Even if you don't want to be, you are likely to be laid transparent—for better or worse. Indeed, when clusters of trust form, they are likely to be increasingly reinforced. Cloud-based virtual filters for the physical world will create an increased reliance on direct advice from trusted advisors at the point of purchase. Indeed, most people will have a virtual overlay on their experience of the physical world when they are shopping.

For its part, the organization that does not understand the diaspora-driven differences between these two consumers will be, at best, confused by how to communicate its own values and, at worst, deeply counterproductive to its own interests.

Organizations must work to understand their own values first. And those organizations that understand the various value clusters among their consumers and earn their trust by working with those values in mind will find the wind at their backs. We are well on the way to the emergence of a whole category of retailers that emphasize values and rights-of-way. Companies such as Apple, REI, and Whole Foods have taken the concept of networks of trust to almost evangelical levels and have been rewarded with fierce loyalty. These companies have permission to play and innovate—as long as they stay on their home court and keep delivering.

For brands that understand networks of trust, the customer will be king—but smart companies will redefine *customers* as a network of trust in their brand. Diasporas will lavish rewards on those brands that they feel to be working in cooperation with their own values, but they will sharply punish those organizations that are seen as failing to live up to those values. Networks of trust will shape how rights-of-way are perceived and accepted. To develop a business based on these partnerships, a company needs to nurture—constantly and fervently—the trust of those it wishes to serve.

Values-driven high-trust brands will be able to charge a hefty premium over competitors with transactional products and utilitarian service. The flip side, however, is that brands that are seen as violating this trust will have hell to pay. See, for example, how Apple had to answer for working conditions in China. Whole Foods was put on the defense when founder John Mackey argued against the Obama administration's health care plan in an op ed. Just as consumers have increasingly found the network on their shoulders advising their day-to-day purchase decisions, companies in the future will increasingly be looking over their own shoulders to gauge their networks' reactions to decisions that in the past would not have been considered customer relevant. Trust will be difficult to grow, but easy to violate. And in the world of social media, big brands will often be accused falsely of violations in trust.

In a socialstructed world, partners will come from anywhere and they could be any size. Collaboration, teaming, and partnerships will become possible on a scale that could never before have been imagined. Start building trust today to open up your future possibilities for partnering.

Partnering for scalable reciprocity will be a way to learn about new markets, a way to accomplish what you could not alone, a way to lower your innovation risk, a way to have broader impacts, and a healthier way to live and do business.

CHAPTER 7

How Gameful Engagement Will Disrupt Experimenting to Learn

Stretching and learning
using emotion-laden
attention, to grow

———

Games are obstacles we volunteer to overcome.

JANE MCGONIGAL,
Reality Is Broken

———

Think ahead ten years—how will corporations experiment to learn about the business they want to create? In other words, how will you prototype your new business? The answer: you will game it. And you can start now.

In order to learn how to make money in new ways, you will need to get others gamefully engaged with your idea. Often, you will need to give away assets from your existing right-of-way in order to engage people and in order to learn how to make money in new ways.

The subtitle of Jane McGonigal's marvelous book *Reality Is Broken* is *Why Games Make Us Better and How They Can Change the World*. As we look ahead at learning by experimenting over the next decade, we have to think about gaming as a way of engaging more and more people to help them work toward better and better worlds. Scalability reciprocity can be a means to a better world, but it will require engagement. How might you get people engaged? You make it fun.

You make it meaningful. You lower risks by simulating, rather than playing for real right away.

Games are first-person stories that can allow traditionally impersonalized situations to be less alienating. For example, gameful competition has successfully been used in call centers to make the repetitive task of answering consumer inquiries less tedious. Callers unlock new privileges with specific positive behaviors, and an underlying architecture of deeper interpersonal connection and meaning is projected onto a task. United Health has experimented with this approach and found that it increased efficiency. This economy of engagement is also an economy in which positive feelings—pride, curiosity, love, and feeling smart—are the ultimate reward for participation.

The content range of video games is expanding beyond shooting games to include games that are more wholesome, more business-like, and more meaningful. But however you feel about the content of today's video games, consider the quality of the human-computer interface that the video gaming industry is creating. Gameful engagement will get more people involved, and that engagement can be constructive. Gameful engagement can give people a sense of meaning and purpose. It all depends on what sorts of games you choose to play.

In the next ten years, gameful engagement will provide much better ways to get many more people engaged—on a global scale. Socially constructive games—such as the University of Washington's FoldIt and UCLA Biogames that we discussed in Chapter 3—will blossom into much more sophisticated forms of gameful engagement.

Consider how a FoldIt-like game could develop over the next ten years. New product or service ideas could be prototyped gamefully, with input from players around the world. Potential customers could get involved in the design of the basic concepts, rather than just buying the finished product. This vision of gameful engagement—engagement with the brand—will take companies into the space that was formerly occupied by marketing organizations.

People, and kids especially, have always played games, and those games have always provided emotionally enhanced experiences. But digital technology has changed games. The tools for emotional enhancement have never been so rich—and they will get much richer. Games are not new. What's new are the *interfaces* and *connectivity*. Today's games are immersive, but they are only market tests for even more vivid forms of immersion and engagement yet to come.

Gameful engagement has already gotten interesting, but in this next decade, it will become ubiquitous and even more engaging.

The digital natives will create some of these experiences themselves, but they will also purchase them. To reach digital natives companies will need not only engagement, but *gameful* engagement. As we proposed in Chapter 5, the term *gameful engagement* is a more appropriate alternative for the current concepts of marketing, advertising, and commercials.

We don't recommend using the term *gamification*, since it is likely that gaming will be oversold and used by marketing organizations to manipulate the people who use their products. *Gamification* is coming to mean adding a touch of gaming to something you are already doing—it is the horseless carriage equivalent of gameful engagement. Certainly, there will be a backlash against gamification, but the underlying value of gameful engagement will be enduring.

Economist Edward Castranova studies massively multiplayer online games (MMOs) that engage their players for an average of 21 hours per week. He identifies "positive emotions"—rather than escapism, competition, or entertainment—as the single most important motivation for playing. He argues that most players turn to games specifically to produce the emotional high associated with accomplishing something concrete, feeling capable, and being recognized for their successes. Castranova has found, for example, that he can induce positive emotions by having players engage in simple tasks that offer an experience of success. For example, it has been found that playing video games with the difficulty level set to *easy* can be an effective treatment for depression for some people.

According to game designers and social media researchers, to engage the widest possible user base, you have to accept that there is no typical participant in any given online community. Instead, there exist multiple participant types. These types vary according to two important factors: what the participant wants and how much the participant is willing to contribute.

Games designed to appeal across these differences will be able to achieve maximum engagement and may in many cases remake the institutions and codes governing society. There are, however, dangers here. If a game is perceived as manipulative or does not engage in a genuinely meaningful way, gamification efforts could backfire. The term of art for this reaction is *badge fatigue,* based on typical reactions to poorly designed game systems that award players essentially meaningless merit badges for performing more or less arbitrary tasks.

Military Gaming

Bob was invited with a group of business leaders to visit the US Army War College in Carlisle, Pennsylvania, where he observed how the military uses games to help people learn and experiment in first-person and extremely realistic ways.

Without a military background, this was a whole new experience for Bob, and he went in skeptically. He had heard that the Army War College, the Army's graduate school for future generals, was the slowest moving, most hierarchical, and least innovative of all the military graduate schools. He was surprised and impressed, however, when—just after 9/11—the Army War College started referring to itself informally as VUCA University (for Volatile, Uncertain, Complex, and Ambiguous).

Since 9/11, Bob has returned to the Army War College many times to lead exchanges between business, nonprofit, and military leaders, and he teaches there periodically to share IFTF's latest forecasts. From these experiences he has learned that Army War College pedagogy makes heavy use of gaming and immersive learning, which means that the military is better prepared for the digital natives than other educational institutions or corporations. The military is at the leading edge of gameful engagement, and corporations can learn from them.

One of the exchanges that Bob facilitated at Carlisle Barracks focused on gaming. Attendees included video game designers, military war gamers, and business gamers. Their language and approaches varied dramatically. Video game designers spend much more time and money to create elegant and strikingly vivid computer interface designs than do companies or the military.

The military, on the other hand, invests much more in realism. For example, Bob participated in a global crisis simulation with Afghan actors, real news reporters, and actual members of Congress. The simulation was very realistic due to the staging and human actors, even though the computer interfaces were not very impressive.

In general, the corporate gamers were behind both the military and the video game designers. Only a few businesses make sophisticated use of gaming. Medical schools and hospitals, however, are big users of simulation for training. If there is a chance that people will die, there is real incentive to game it in advance in order to reduce that risk.

Bob also visited the National Training Center (NTC) for the Army in the Mojave Desert, which is the last stop for troops before going to war. At about the size of the state of Rhode Island, the NTC is essentially the world's largest video gaming parlor. Participants come in groups and play war games that could last for two weeks, 24 hours a day. The design philosophy is to make the experience harder than real warfare. Many people are killed during games without actually having to die.

Bob got to interview the virtually dead on the battlefield. They were having the first-person learning experiences of their lifetimes. The villages were quite realistic, and the scripts were demanding.

Imagine how immersive learning experiences might be used to prepare people for the future in business. Such experiences could provide rising star leaders with a chance to practice in a low-risk way, to get a sense of the VUCA World of the future before the stakes become real.

The best way to prepare for the future is to immerse yourself in it. There are many things that companies can do now to learn from the digital natives and learn how to gamefully engage with them.

The game Spore is a virtual immersion in nature. Created by iconic game designer Will Wright (creator of SimCity, The Sims, and many other socially constructive games) and published by Electronic Arts (EA), Spore embodies the principles of biology, much as earlier games embodied the principles of engineering. Parents who are lucky are able to play Spore with their kids and learn systems biology at the same time. Players generate creatures starting from one-celled organisms up through civilizations.

Reciprocity is already common practice in many forms of online gaming, and in this spirit, fellow gamers create the content of Spore. There are no expectations of quid pro quo exchange among the players, but the general mood is "play it forward," which contributes to the ongoing game. This lack of expectation is what makes reciprocity different from purely transactional relationships.

In *Leaders Make the Future*, Bob describes the leadership skill of *bio-empathy*: the ability to learn from the principles of nature and apply them in your own leadership. Gameful engagement will give leaders a new tool set for learning and applying the principles of nature on a very large scale.

In ten years, the top leaders in the top companies will all be gamers in some sense of the word. Today's video games only hint at where we are going, but certainly the VUCA World will embrace immersive learning and gameful engagement. Law enforcement, the medical community, fire services, and the military are all far ahead of business with regard to using games and immersive learning.. All leaders need to learn how to gamefully engage—while realizing that there is much we cannot control.

Is "Game" the Best Word?

The word *game* is problematic. In some companies, the word *game* just doesn't work. IFTF recently designed a game for senior executives in a large corporation, for example, but the company didn't want to call it a *game*. This was a very serious company and its leaders didn't want their people "playing games" instead of working. We called our game an *immersive scenario*, and it was a big success.

We expect that the word *game* will become more acceptable within business cultures, but it may take time. The key element is first-person immersive experiences, rather than the usual third-person learning associated with lectures or training programs. We like the term *gameful engagement*, since it emphasizes the playful element but also the necessity for first-person engagement.

For some people, the word *simulation* is much more respectable. The distinction between *simulation* and *gaming* is not precise or consistent, but simulations do tend to be more serious and reality based than games. While games emphasize experiencing alternative environments and experimenting with novel behaviors, simulation is typically about creating an environment where actions have an impact that's as close as possible to reality.

There are two common problems in the applications of business metrics: either the wrong things are measured, or the existing measurements are used in the wrong way, both yielding poor decisions. Depending on how it's applied, simulation could serve as either an aggravator or a corrective for this tendency. Thus, it is important to be sure that one is simulating the right system with the right degree of granularity in order to make wiser decisions. Models based on incomplete data caused Wall Street quants to dramatically misprice subprime mortgages, a cautionary example of what happens when sloppy simulation feeds real-world decision making.

In many ways, gameful engagement and simulation overlap, and it is not difficult to imagine a world in which realistic simulations rely on game interfaces to maximize employee performance in certain areas. In any case, new interfaces will improve users' experiences so much that gameful engagement and simulations are likely approaching a golden age.

Simulation can be simply defined as the creation of realistic models in which it is possible to prototype new approaches and explore for new interconnections. Data-based simulation is all about playing out the connections within a system in a realistic way. When done well, it is a tool for communicating as well as for forecasting. If you can simulate a system, you can project it forward. This forecasting is the basis of a certain kind of strategic futures thinking, in which scenarios can be used to construct new opportunities for business growth and even for setting one's business vision. Projects optimized in this way have been stress tested to increase their market potential.

Business applications of this kind of simulation could allow for more accurate predictions of shopper behavior, not only of what they might buy but also which goods drive their interest.

Gaming Your Way to a New Business

The next decade will be boiling with emotionally enhanced attention that will allow companies—indeed *require* companies—to rethink how they experiment to learn and ultimately how they do marketing, advertising, and commercials.

Corporations will need to engage in playful and authentic ways. Commercials and advertising as we know them will cease to exist and will be replaced with exchanges that are more personalized, playful, and engaging.

What corporations tell people will become less important than what people tell each other about corporations and their products.

Corporations will need to learn about new business opportunities by using game-like approaches to try them out in low-risk ways. They will need to engage with their customers—especially the digital natives—not just market to them. They will need to learn how to experiment to learn, in a spirit of gameful engagement.

CHAPTER 8

How Cloud-Served Supercomputing Will Disrupt the Practice of Scaling

**Cloud will amplify
and propagate new business
innovate and scale**

The network is the computer.

JOHN GAGE

John Gage was the first person we ever heard talk about the network *being* the computer. It was the 1980s, Bob recalls, when Gage first said, "The network is the computer," and it was a visionary aspiration back then. At that time, John Gage was the chief scientist at Sun Microsystems. (This is also when Eric Schmidt was the chief technologist at Sun—long before he went to Google as CEO and led Google's push to create cloud-served supercomputing.)

Within the next decade, it finally will become true: the network *will* be the computer and cloud-served supercomputing will become a reality. As the network becomes the computer, the ability to scale will be amplified dramatically.

The boundaries between consumer and producer will be further blurred by the dynamics of cloud-amplified leapfrog innovation. Just as producers will be able to closely coordinate supplier resources using the cloud, consumers will too. Digital matchmaking has already opened up some intriguing possibilities, such as Chinese tuángòus and buying cooperatives such as Groupon going mainstream. Within this context, consumers will be able to express individual preferences and have these aggregated in the cloud. When a particular innovation appeals to enough potential customers, this pent-up demand can automatically trigger the production process instead of the other way around.

Cloud-Served Supercomputing

Like so many other emerging technologies in the past, the cloud has been oversold and—so far—has underdelivered. That, however, is about to change. The cloud is not just about outsourcing information technology functions and providing storage. Soon the cloud will function like a supercomputer, providing a virtual·overlay on the physical world to allow us to do things we've never done before. This cloud-served supercomputer will allow us to scale and propagate in ways we have never before imagined.

Cloud-served supercomputing will be characterized by dramatically increased global connectivity, with parallel processing power that will be available to a much larger portion of the world's population. Expect powerful amplification of almost everything, with public demands for transparency and grating uncertainty about privacy. The cloud will amplify reciprocity *and* it will introduce new risks of criminal hacking

New economic practices based on sharing, bartering, lending, trading, gifting, and reciprocity will become much easier in the cloud. Indeed, cloud-served supercomputing will amplify these new economic models and drive them to scale. Scalable reciprocity will attract a wide-ranging mix of players to create extraordinary growth and scaling opportunities. In a way, social media is a return to kinship-based cultures—but on a larger and more virtual scale.[39]

Cloud-served supercomputing will be characterized by

- global and increasingly open access;
- multimedia and multilingual capabilities;
- increasingly mobile access;
- links to sensors that will be cheap, ubiquitous, and often connected (some of which will be in our bodies);
- filters of the physical world, using a range of criteria and offered by a wild mix of players;
- flexibility in ways that we can only imagine now;
- lower costs for computing and communications (although costs for services and experiences will vary greatly and may become increasingly expensive).

From a consumer products standpoint, we are within a decade of cloud-based coordination that could, for example, facilitate self-organizing supply chains or bring insights from the most sophisticated business analytics engines to the local street-corner market in Delhi. Amplified by the cloud, people with initiative and energy to innovate can bring themselves up to speed—using the most powerful business tools in existence—no matter where they happen to live.

Essentially the same dynamic plays itself out on a generational level as we move into a world where it is possible for families to routinely move themselves from being premodern agrarians all the way to sophisticated cloud-served regional moguls inside of a generation. Indeed, in this environment, cultural values and accumulated wisdom may be more important than ever as regional infrastructure and innovations become relatively less important. It will be those communities that emphasize virtues of personal self-discipline and wise management that will succeed, rather than those that seek to leverage the infrastructure and innovations established by previous generations. In a leapfrog world, there will be fewer opportunities to rest on past laurels. Track records, however, will be important. Both good and bad deeds will be stored in the cloud.

The cost of innovation will fall dramatically because of the cloud. Just a few years ago, even in Silicon Valley, it was expensive to start a new company. One of the major expenses in those days was a server. Now, you can have a startup idea in the morning, buy cloud-computing services, and be online by evening. Similarly, the cost of scaling will fall too.

Cloud-served supercomputing will fuel global innovation and propagation—especially in emerging markets. In a world where the network becomes the computer, practical supercomputing resources will become available to anyone, anyplace, anytime. Infrastructure in emerging markets could leapfrog capabilities in the so-called developed world—just as cell phone technology leapfrogged traditional landlines. Small players will get access to large resources regardless of where they are. New connections will be made, connections that have never been drawn before.

Rapid Propagation, Amplified by the Cloud

While it is tempting to imagine that leapfrog innovations are nearly always in the digital domain, many digital innovations have very real offline implications. For example, the Chinese company Yihaodian has managed to attract the attention of some of the world's largest producers by offering Chinese consumers access to an inventory of thousands of groceries and consumer goods online. While logistical realities still constrain this approach from becoming the dominant consumer experience—even in the developed world—it is clear that further disruption will occur.

Thus, it is easy to imagine the enterprising entrepreneurs of tomorrow cautiously approaching their next innovations by first asking relevant networks of people if they would be willing to buy a currently unavailable product if it were to be produced. When enough people answer yes, a limited-risk production process could be automatically triggered. Indeed early forms of exactly this model are already beginning to take hold on sites such as Kickstarter or Indiegogo. For those used to the idea that the entrepreneur is a heroic risk-taker, the possibility of innovation itself as a utility is a fascinating alternative. Inventors, entrepreneurs, and makers will be increasingly able to go directly to the crowd to identify potential customers and even fund their innovations.

TED used the early cloud to amplify its brand globally through TEDx licenses. Because TED continues to host in-person conferences, it is both in the cloud and in the physical world—another example of the world of And, not Or.

The TEDx experience will be tame compared to what will become possible. Expect far more impressive expressions of digital leapfrogging in the coming years as digital technologies transform many of today's fixed costs of business into variable pay-as-you go utilities. Simply by giving emerging regions direct access to the increasing returns being offered by Moore's Law over the coming decades, cloud computing could make the proliferation of cell phones look slow.

Neuroscience in the Cloud

Human history has been defined by our eagerness to merge with our tools, actively seeking out ways to extend the mind. We created writing to make our thoughts concrete and portable. Assistive technologies from eyeglasses to hearing aids have extended human vision, hearing, and other senses, augmenting our abilities to perceive the world. Our machines crunch numbers at rates much faster than we can. We have coevolved with our technologies—and we will continue to do so.

Neuroscience and neurotechnology will soon get practical—with great potential for commercial innovation—but it will come with great risks of being misunderstood. The next one hundred years will be the century of the brain. Over the next decade, we will see the early fruits of this transition with much deeper understanding of how our brains work and how they shape, enhance, and limit our behavior. The result may be nothing less than a new science of persuasion. Neuroscience in commercial innovation, however, will be a slippery slope. The potential to understand shoppers' brains will grow, but at the risk of corporations being perceived as heartless manipulators.

The higher ground here is personal choice. If companies can use neuroscience to help people make their own choices, this is likely to be welcomed. If neuroscience is used in manipulative ways to get people to buy or do things, it will be resisted.

In the past, the findings of neuroscience have been largely academic in scope, but they are now becoming practical. In recent years, these findings have begun to trickle down into popular self-help books, particularly those that emphasize the process of "rewiring" one's brain based on the science of neuroplasticity—the brain's ability to adapt and change based on experience, even in later life.

In short, how we think about thinking will change—and this goes beyond a new sense of neuroplasticity. We are coming to understand that mental processes once deemed as constrained to the brain or the mind are in fact deeply shaped by the world around us. Over time, these changes will profoundly affect how we design our institutions, organizations, and communications. In the next decade, we will offload more and more of our cognitive processes to our devices, our networks, and our built environments. Those who take advantage of insights emerging at the intersections of cognitive sciences, behavioral sciences, and human-computer interaction will be able to harness and direct the outcomes of human thought with greater precision and power.

Most of us intuitively still see our brains and the outside world as independent components, which we hope work in concert but not as a functional unit. However, the increasing integration of our minds with machines and the blending of our online and offline realities are giving many of us the everyday experience of a kind of cognitive comingling with our technologies.

It is likely that as a result of growing neurological understanding, organizations will have a deeper understanding of consumer behavior. However, parallel to this is an increased risk that those who use these tools could be violating trust. Right now we see only the outcomes of shopping, not the true underlying behavior. Currently we can only dimly understand how people make decisions and deal with complexity. To the degree that shopping is the process of considering and acquiring goods and services to meet needs and wants, these insights could fundamentally transform the shopping experience.

The knowledge economy is well into maturity, and the creative economy is not far behind, yet our work processes, places, and spaces still reflect an industrial-design model. As we begin to understand how to best organize workflows for the way our brains actually work, we will see radical changes in business. Cloud-served supercomputing will amplify the socialstructing possibilities we discussed in Chapter 5.

At a minimum, we are learning how much our distractions and information overloads inhibit the kind of focus needed for many of the mental tasks we are asked to do throughout the day. Organizations will be looking for ways to reduce these. Agents in our computers and communication devices could curate the flow of information in ways that manage any distractions that increase our cognitive load or decrease our productivity.

Yet, not all knowledge work is the same. There are times in the course of the day or course of a project when certain cognitive skills are needed more than others. We already know the importance of setting the right vibe for brainstorming, or critical feedback, or logistical discussions. Our environments will become our cognitive aids in these processes. Businesses and groups will consider which spaces lend themselves to certain kinds of thinking and adjust their environments accordingly. In short, practices around what might be called *cognitive ergonomics* will enter the workplace lexicon.

The cloud is essentially an amplifier for our brains—and our emerging collective brain. It will allow many new possibilities, and it will allow innovation to happen much more quickly. The next ten years will be disruptive, a break in the pattern of network evolution that began in 1968 when the ARPAnet was created. Today's Internet is only a crude test market for tomorrow's cloud-served supercomputing world. The practices of propagation will be disrupted in powerful ways.

The Multilingual Cloud

Localized cloud access will become a commercial innovation medium. The English-language Internet is what most people think of as "The Internet," but the Chinese-language Internet is almost as large. Multilingual tools will facilitate greater connections between these largely autonomous networks, increasing cross-fertilization of ideas. Commercial innovators should experiment with new ways to connect to global Internet users and to engage with them. There is much to be learned from niche markets whose insights and best practices will suddenly become comprehensible on an international scale. The future will be unevenly distributed, and it may just pass by those who fail to pay attention to the full spectrum of global communications. A world of many Ands.

These localized domains will allow smaller communities to have a place to self-identify and promote their language, which will increase their online comfort level. This should also offer countless new opportunities and benefits for Internet users around the world to establish and use domains in their native language. However, internationalized domain names will complement the current top-level domains, not fully take their place. An increase in localized websites represents the opening of a market that is eager and ready to be on the Internet. New partnering models will become possible, *And* partnering through these new domains will be complicated.

Few of the world's languages have the language-specific knowledge resources that English does. A great number of these are minority languages, which becomes obvious when one compares the number of languages to the number of countries. And most minority languages are not taught in schools.

Yet, when taught in their own language, students readily transfer literacy skills to the languages used in education, acquiring essential tools for lifelong learning. This results in higher self-esteem and a community that is better equipped to communicate with the rest of the world.

Given the enormous lead it already enjoys and its increasing use as a lingua franca in other spheres, English web content may continue to dominate the Internet even as other languages claim their stakes. This is a classic positive feedback loop: new Internet users find it helpful to learn English and employ it online, thus reinforcing the language's prestige and forcing subsequent new users to learn English as well.

Certain other factors have contributed to English being the dominant language on the web. Most notable in this regard is the tendency for researchers and professionals to publish in English to ensure maximum exposure. The largest database of medical bibliographical information, for example, reveals that English was the majority language choice for the past forty years, and its share has continually increased over the same period.

It is clear that when people are able to type a .com domain in their own native language, it makes connecting with them a great deal easier and would give a huge advantage to companies that provide that option. Take, for instance, סיבלכ.com (Dogs.com in Hebrew). It would be even easier if Israel had a localized top-level domain such as "לי." (".IL"), so users wouldn't have to transition back and forth between English and Hebrew when typing the domain.

Indeed, many people are more comfortable formulating search queries in their own language than typing them into Google. To overcome this difficulty, some people have resorted to copying and pasting from other sites or from online translation tools.

The changes in the architecture of the Internet will be further amplified by a number of other technologies. Foremost among these is the capability to translate languages, made possible by cloud-served translation systems. The technology behind these systems is machine learning, which works by statistically analyzing thousands of documents. Partnering across languages will become much more feasible in this cloud-served world.

For speakers of languages that either have no written form or are difficult to enter by keyboard, direct speech inputs could enable them to interact with the Internet through voice recognition systems and speech translation. Indeed, voice-in/voice-out interfaces are now beginning to make their way to market for English speakers. Without the burden of translating, new markets will open instantly.

Faster and Further

Researchers and makers are also exploring the potential of socialbot swarms to stretch and amplify global work organizations. Socialbots are semi-autonomous computer programs that work in concert with humans in social networks. Think of socialbots as potential nonhuman partners or participants. Socialbot swarms will be able to accomplish what humans alone cannot and can be used to create scalable reciprocity.

Socialbot swarms will live in the cloud and create new ways to grow and achieve scale globally. The railroads and telegraph companies didn't have the cloud, but they did have early connectivity that was able to amplify whatever they did locally. What if they had asked larger questions, instead of just focusing on the transactional value of the new technology to incrementally improve old businesses? The communications companies of today will have to address this change or become irrelevant.

Think of the cloud as a medium for growing shared assets, or commons. Commons creating is the most advanced of the ten future leadership skills discussed in *Leaders Make the Future*. Commons creating is the ability to seed, nurture, and grow shared assets that can benefit all players—and allow competition at a higher lever.[40]

Moving forward, expect industries to reshape themselves using more lightweight models and approaches. A few key tools with specific capabilities—both organizational and technological—are emerging that will allow organizations to experiment with these lightweight models of innovation.

The best way to think about the cloud will be as an amplifier, a very large and sometimes unpredictable amplifier. Whatever you do, for good or for evil, will be amplified by the cloud. Amplification is at the root of scalability. Amplification accelerates propagation.

Everyone will need a filter in the world of the cloud. Think of the cloud as a virtual overlay on the physical world with amazing supercomputer capabilities that will help people make sense out of the complexities around them.

Cloud-served supercomputing will play a big role in how reciprocity advantage plays out over the next decade. Your reciprocity advantage will be empowered and amplified through the cloud.

How to Develop Your Own Reciprocity Advantage

The hardest part of thinking about the future is figuring out what to do next—given the external future forces. In other words: "How do I make this foresight actionable?"

The purpose of forecasting is to make better decisions in the present. Even though ten-year forecasting is actually easier than one- or two-year forecasting, it is very hard to draw out practical insights and actions. In Part Three we focus on helping you draw out your own insights and actions, so that you can make better decisions.

Part Three is in a workshop format, with questions and templates that take you through each of the four steps and help you create your own reciprocity advantage that can scale massively.

Many people mistakenly think that invention is random. While not completely predictable, the reality is that to innovate you must choose where you want to go but then be flexible about how to get there. Serial inventors have developed repeatable processes that they may or may not be able to articulate. As the world's most prolific inventor, Thomas Edison, observed, "Invention is one-percent inspiration and ninety-nine percent perspiration."

Successful innovators ask questions that help nurture new business. Each chapter in Part Three highlights the questions you must ask—and answer—in order to create a reciprocity advantage:

Chapter 9. How can you uncover your own right-of-way? Answering this question will require you to assess your current core business. It is through understanding your core business more clearly that you will find the assets you want to leverage. Every company is in at least three industries. That third industry is where you can create a reciprocity advantage. Consider these questions to stretch your thinking about your right-of-way:

1. What industry are you in with the current products you sell?

2. If you were to offer a service, what industry would you be in?

3. If you were to offer an experience, what industry would you be in?

Chapter 10. How can you find the best partners for you? Chapter 10 will help you find the common ground that brings you together with a partner. This will be essential to weather all the other differences that exist between the two of you. Ask yourself these questions:

1. What is it that I've always wanted to do, but couldn't do without a partner?

2. Is this the best partner with whom I could share my right-of-way?

3. Will this new partnership be able to succeed on a large scale?

Chapter 11. How can you learn by experimenting? The biggest mistake in creating a new business is not planning how to scale it from the beginning. We will encourage you to imagine your idea as the next billion-dollar business! If you are a big company or expecting a venture capital firm to back you, a billion dollars is the minimum threshold for a new global market. If you are small, focusing on a billion-dollar prize will open your mind to the real issues. Ask these questions:

1. What has to be true for this to be a billion-dollar business?

2. What are the two killer issues you must answer in order to achieve that goal?

3. Do you have the work process to do hundreds—or even thousands—of prototypes per month?

Chapter 12. How can you scale your reciprocity advantage? Successful new business ideas will be desirable, viable, and ownable: someone wants it, you know how to make money at it, and you will be able to win when competition enters. Your experiments should continue until all three are true. Small is beautiful until you have this answer. Then, go big and go fast. This will be the time to stop experimenting and scale massively.

1. Is your idea desirable?

2. Is your idea viable?

3. Is your idea ownable?

In his iconic book *Innovator's Dilemma,* Clayton Christensen observed that time and again leading companies failed to see the impending threat that little companies posed until it was too late to do anything. Christensen concentrated on the minimills that displaced giants like US Steel and the minicomputers that made mainframes obsolete. Incremental innovation happens within the confines of a current business, but disruptive innovation breaks beyond those bounds. Reciprocity advantage will break beyond the bounds of current thinking.

When Karl was at Procter & Gamble leading disruptive innovation efforts to create new businesses, he would jokingly say that he would prefer Clay Christensen's job to his own. After all, Professor Christensen did post mortems on dead companies to determine the cause of each one's untimely demise. Businessman Ronn had to create new businesses, while also keeping the current business growing year after year after year. Although doctors probably shouldn't operate on themselves, businesses are required to in order to thrive, even though it is particularly risky in disruptive innovation spaces.

In a giant company such as P&G, most people work on the core businesses—and that's exactly what they should be doing. They need to work hard to keep the more than $80 billion in sales from declining. The growth in these businesses tends to be small, hard fought, and incremental. To find new business, however, you have to look in other places and ask different questions.

P&G was not looking for Swiffer when it was created. Rather, P&G knew there was not enough money in selling liquid in a bottle under the Mr. Clean brand to meet their growth goals. Gordon Brunner, P&G's Chief Technical Officer at the time, made a radical decision. He took away all the R&D funding for Mr. Clean but then gave it back on one condition—that the team create a product other than liquid in a bottle. The result was a new product design that they first thought of as a mop—not a liquid in a bottle. Within a year, the definition of what came to be called Swiffer was taking shape. Brunner forced them to ask different questions in order to provoke a new kind of product.

Febreze has a similar history. P&G had more than $10 billion in detergent sales. All these businesses had one thing in common: clothes were washed in a washing machine. Nabil Sakaab, the innovation leader for the business, needed new growth. His team observed: "Ninety-nine percent of clothes were laundered, but as much money was spent on the other one percent." For ten dollars you could wash hundreds of garments and towels *or* with the same ten dollars you could dry-clean a single jacket. What if P&G could clean that one garment without putting it in the machine? Shortly, Febreze was born using the existing technology that P&G had already created for Bounce dryer sheets. Sakaab asked a question that hadn't been asked before, and again, a brand new product was born.

Mark Schar, a former P&G executive who went on to earn a PhD at Stanford after his business career, has coined the term *pivot thinking* to describe this ability to pivot from one way of thinking to another in an effort to see new innovation opportunities.[41] We all need to develop our own pivot skills, and asking different questions is a great way to get started.

We invite you to turn to your own company, ask different questions, and get started on the journey toward creating your own reciprocity advantage.

CHAPTER 9

How to Uncover Your Right-of-Way

The best way to predict the future is to invent it.

ALAN KAY,
when he was at Xerox PARC

Right-of-way is grounded in the assets, relationships, and investments you have already made to run your current business in your current industry. Reciprocity advantage offers a new way to get value from your underutilized strengths to create a new business.

What underutilized assets do you have? If someone comes to you with an idea for making money with something you aren't currently monetizing, it is worth a discussion. If the idea is one that complements your business and offers an opportunity to make money in new ways, it is a great lead. If it is an idea that uses your assets to make money that you could make on your own, however, it should just become part of your core business—not a reciprocity advantage.

The biggest missed rights-of-way in the 2000s involved social media. All successful brands and big companies have millions of loyal users, but most of them use only those databases to sell the same customers more of the same product in the same ways. However, such networks of users could be an invaluable right-of-way.

Twitter, for example, hit smack in the middle of CNN's right-of-way. Twitter now provides a medium for tracking rapidly unfolding crisis events—just the kind of events that CNN is so good at tracking and reporting in great detail. Now, CNN chases Twitter and builds it into its reporting. It is too late for CNN to buy Twitter. CNN should have developed Twitter or it could have bought it early, but now it has to adapt and catch up. CNN missed an important part of its own right-of-way.

Similarly, Tumblr developed in Yahoo's right-of-way. Yahoo should have developed Tumblr or bought it early. Instead it paid over a billion dollars for the popular social network, and Yahoo's CEO was forced to say sheepishly, "We won't screw it up." That is embarrassing for Yahoo, but so instructive for companies seeking to uncover their own rights-of-way before others do. You don't want to be in a situation where you are forced to overpay for something that was in your right-of-way in the first place.

The value of existing networks is now becoming clear in the big data disruption of this decade. People are crunching the numbers to discover new insights to sell them new kinds of products, services, or experiences—and in more ways.

The challenge for a company is to embrace the disruptions. TED saw the social revolution and created TEDx. IBM saw burgeoning data and created Smarter Planet. Microsoft relented to the users and made Kinect the new platform for gestural interfaces.

How Do You Find Your Right-of-Way?

Finding your right-of-way will require a deep understanding of your business—beyond day-to-day operations. Rethinking your business will open your management team's eyes to new possibilities.

The process we use to help companies has three steps and is done in a workshop format. We involve the senior leaders from the company in a one-day session where they collaborate to do the three-step portfolio assessment process. We force them to map all their projects using the nine-box matrix to assess their innovation portfolios. Essentially we ask them to create their equivalent of the analysis that the railroad companies wished they had made.

The first stage in finding your right-of-way has three parts:

1. **Begin by defining your core business**. This is where you will find the right-of-way assets you can share. Not all should be shared. You must do this inventory and then decide later what to keep and what to share.

2. **Reinvent your business as a service**. Stepping back to generalize your business will help you see possible disruptions that could obsolete your core. The rights-of-way that your core needs to survive disruption are not to be shared. This would hurt your business. Instead, invest to prevent long-term obsolescence.

3. **Redefine your business as an experience**. Having attained clarity on what you do as a service, focus on the users of your service. What are you being hired to do? By looking for services that people want but don't yet have, you will find new ways to compete that *complement*, rather than *compete with*, your core business. The rights-of-way that enable this are the core of the new reciprocity business.

The search is structured to follow specific steps, but the discussion is what matters. Part Three is structured in a workshop style that is designed to start good conversations. Figure 7 is a summary of the process we recommend for uncovering your right-of-way.

FINDING YOUR RIGHT-OF-WAY

Each of your current innovation projects will fall into one of the nine boxes. If a project falls into two boxes, divide it into separate projects. A single project that runs across multiple boxes is not likely to succeed. The team members or their management will be at odds with each other as the project progresses. Divide the project and then choose where to put the priority when you split projects, but don't allow individual projects to fall across the lines.

Again, the most important part of this exercise will be the dis-

Commercial and Technical Uncertainty	1st Industry	2nd Industry	3rd Industry
High	Major replatforming	Inventing new technology to obsolete the core	Emerging science or technology that would need your right-of-way
Medium	Major upgrades	Reapplying technology to obsolete or complement the core	Using your right-of-way and existing technology to create new businesses
Low	Incremental improvements	Using existing technology to complement the core	Using your right-of-way and existing technology to create new business

	1st Industry	2nd Industry	3rd Industry
What industry are you in?	Our product	Our service	Our experience
The innovation challenge	Maintain healthy core business	Reinvent how you do the core	Use your right-of-way

Figure 7: Finding Your Right-of-Way.

cussion. Remember, there will not be just one answer. Create many different maps if you wish. Then get your senior management group together to determine which ones you want to pursue.

RIGHT-OF-WAY STEP 1:
AGREE ON YOUR CORE BUSINESS

Do an experiment for yourself. Ask this question of ten people in various parts of your company: "What industry are we in?

Chances are you will get a wide range of answers, from the very specific to the very general. In most companies, there is little clarity around what seems to be such a basic question.

What industry *are* you in? The objective answer can be found by

---

TIPS FOR IDENTIFYING YOUR CURRENT INDUSTRY

These are investments you must make to stay ahead of current competition.

- Where do you make two-thirds of your money? This is your core business.

- A narrow definition is better than a broad one. This is what you are known for. This is the business you will defend, no matter what.

- Your business is part of a bigger industry. Rules are changed at the industry level. The industry is a global set of competitors with at least $10 billion in annual sales.

- Even if you are small, find a set of competitors whose combined sales are in the $10 billion range. You need to know whom you compete against or you will be easily blindsided by competitors moving into your geography.

- Diversified companies might be in multiple industries. Do this exercise for the whole company to find new enterprise-wide businesses. Then do this exercise for each of the business units in nonaligned industries.

- Most innovations are small, but some will require recapitalizing to stay ahead of competition.

---

looking at your sales and profits. What is responsible for two-thirds of your total company's profits or sales? Ignore the rest of your business when you ask this question. Typically one or two product lines and one or two channels or geographies are your core.

Don't worry that the answer to this question will be too narrow. When Karl was in the household cleaning–products business at P&G, they realized they really did only two things: cleaned dishes and floors. Getting really clear on these two businesses allowed them to focus on this core, ignore nonstrategic businesses, and devote efforts to more radical innovations like Swiffer and Febreze.

General Electric (GE) is a huge company. What industry is it in? GE's core industry is infrastructure. It sells aircraft engines, electric power turbines, large diagnostic medical equipment, diesel engines, nuclear reactors, light bulbs, and appliances. While GE sells light bulbs and appliances to consumers, it is not just a consumer company. Its core is huge business-to-business billion-dollar deals.

The core is where you will find your right-of-way for extending into new businesses. And the core will still take the majority of your innovation budget to continuously produce the incremental innovations necessary to stay ahead of competition and to fill all market segments. Keep making your core business better and better. Keep investing in the new technologies to keep ahead of competition. Grow your market share and profitability. Run the best company in your industry.

There's also a practical reason why we start with getting firm agreement on the core business. Without a sound innovation plan for the core business, you will chase the competition and stop all new business efforts when a new product enters the market. New business is not necessarily harder than your existing business, but it must be nurtured with continued support. And you can't nurture new business if you're putting out daily fires in your current business. So fix the core first.

RIGHT-OF-WAY STEP 2:
REINVENT YOUR BUSINESS AS A SERVICE

Ted Levitt, in the landmark *Harvard Business Review* article "Marketing Myopia," observed that the train companies were not just in the train industry—they also were in the transportation industry.[42] His article inspired our railroad model example.

Besides writing in the article about trains, Levitt pointed to electric drills. Why do people use a drill? The answer: they need to make a hole. People who make drills are in the business of making holes.

TIPS FOR IDENTIFYING YOUR SERVICE INDUSTRY

These are investments you must make to prevent your core business from being obsoleted by new competitors.

- What do people hire you to do? Anyone who can do this is a direct competitor.

- Any way that serves your current customers that is orders of magnitude better and cheaper will obsolete your core business over time.

- First versions of the disruption will be crude. Your love of your assets will make you slow to respond.

- Obsolete yourself before others do.

- If you miss the early disruptions, you will have to acquire the companies.

Christensen calls this the "job to be done." Or more commonly, he asks, what job are you being hired to do?

If the first business is drilling holes, the second business is selling anything that makes a hole—even if it requires no drill. We refer to the second industry as a service because it involves hiring you to do the same job you do today but doesn't necessarily use your assets.

Once you have defined your core industry, step back and ask this question: what do people hire us to do?

Forget how you do what you do. Rather, focus on the end result, or the benefit. See the hole—not the drill. Any business that can do what you do—and do it better, faster, or at half the cost—will eventually disrupt you. The good news is that it typically takes ten to twenty years before you become obsolete. Digital will disrupt physical. Smart phone apps have already disrupted single-use devices such as cameras and teleconferencing systems. Why? The incremental cost of a digital transaction is minimal versus the same transaction physically.

The investment in the second industry is complementary to the current investment in the core. Thus, while most of your innovation budget will be spent on the core, about 15 percent of the total innovation investment must be held aside to prevent being obsoleted. You must accomplish this goal for the long run, and it will not be cheap to do. Lead the transition or be run over by it. The railroad companies also needed to get into the airline, trucking, and container-ship businesses because any way that bulk goods or masses of people were moved should have been their kind of business.

It is not optional to get into these service businesses. If there is a business that does what you do a great deal faster or more cheaply, it will eventually be the dominant way of doing business. Rather, you need to make multiple investments in emerging industries that do what you do in radically different ways. This needs to be isolated from the 80 percent of the money that is spent supporting the core, or it will get stolen for short-term fires. As an executive at one company told Karl, "Beware the giant sucking sound of the core."

You will need to keep improving your core business while alternate innovative forms mature. Kodak needed to continue to support silver film for decades, while at the same time it created a new digital business. Over time, the balance of spending will shift toward the disruption, but not for many years. That shift can be difficult, though. Kodak saw the future but never could embrace it. Just as railroad companies loved their trains too much, Kodak loved its silver chemistry too much.

RIGHT-OF-WAY STEP 3:
REDEFINE YOUR BUSINESS AS AN EXPERIENCE

In 1999 Joe Pine was writing about a disruption in how we think about economics and value creation. Pine and his coauthor Jim Gilmore wrote *The Experience Economy: Work Is Theater and Every Business a Stage*. They argued there is a natural progression from products to services to experiences. This perspective was not embraced when the book first came out, but the truth of the argument is now increasingly obvious.

So once you have defined your core business and your service

TIPS FOR IDENTIFYING YOUR EXPERIENCE

These investments create totally incremental, profitable growth made possible by new uses of your existing right-of-way.

- When *aren't* your desired customers hiring you? Consider all times, for all people.

- Focus on nonconsumption; ignore current consumption patterns of your core business. This new business will occur at other times, complementing current consumption patterns.

- Enable people to experience your product's benefits when it is currently impossible to use them.

- Democratize existing desired products and services by substantially reducing the price to meet these needs.

---

industry, ask yourself: if my business were an experience, what industry would I be in?

How often do you get on a train or plane? How many personal business letters do you get through the physical mail? Even if the train companies had invested in planes and trucks, they would have missed the biggest change in the twentieth century—the information and communications revolution.

Imagine a person who lives on the East Coast who has a cousin who lives on the West Coast. At the height of railroad travel, these cousins might have taken the train to visit each other. But because the trip was very long, they rarely saw each other. Commercial airlines shrank the amount of time it took to travel. Planes are the faster version of trains and thus obsoleted railroads as a method to visit distant relatives.

To find this third industry, you need to ask these two cousins what experience they were seeking when they decided to take the train. What did they want to do that caused them to travel? They just wanted to keep in touch. This is what Pine and Gilmore understood—that communication consists of sending words but doesn't necessarily require spending days crossing the country via train.

If you are in the business of moving people, you will argue quite quickly that nothing beats being there in person. It is this kind of logic that most quickly kills new businesses. It is a false dilemma. If you can travel, do so. If you can't travel, then the relevant benchmark is better than doing nothing. Christensen calls this competing against nonconsumption. Something beats nothing most of the time. Only rarely does a new medium replace an old one. Rather, the new medium tends to disrupt the way we use existing media—and those media blend with each other.

Kodak sold cheap cameras at Disneyland because the quality of the picture from your expensive Nikon camera was irrelevant if you forgot to bring it. Blackberry was a very poor machine for doing multipage documents but brilliant for a three-sentence note to get work done before you got back to the office.

The goal of these new-experience businesses is to augment the sales by getting people to pay for things they are not currently buying. Whereas the investments in your new service industries may obsolete your current products, these experience businesses create new markets. So while the new businesses start small, they are nearly 100 percent incremental and can mature into businesses that are much larger than your current company.

Historic Right-of-Way Lessons from the Railroads

Our goal of the three-step process to understanding your business is to help you find the right-of-way that you can share via partnering to create new sources of growth. This is about creating your future. However, a glimpse of the past can help make this more concrete. So, let's now look in detail at how the train business might have evolved.

We know the outcome: the train companies were disrupted by the telegraph. The telegraph enabled the train companies to know exactly where their trains were at any point in time., which allowed them to improve their existing service and to lower the cost. The accounting departments were probably ecstatic because they used the new technology to improve the current business. But they missed the communication revolution, even though they owned the right-of-way for it.

The train companies failed to see that the air rights over their tracks was an asset, so they lost the opportunity to develop telegraphy. Their underutilized asset was the air over their tracks, which was doing nothing for anyone and they were making no money from it. It was there, but they didn't see its potential. When the telegraph people first approached them, the railroad companies should have said something like this: "Tell us more about what you want to do." If the railroads had seen the potential in that asset, they could have had a valuable pathway to growth.

Figure 8 is an example of what the ideal (prescient!) innovation portfolio would have looked like for the railroads industry. The portfolio is a 3-by-3 matrix of innovation investments. Each project a company does will fall into one of the nine boxes. We've filled out the matrix we introduced earlier in this chapter to help you find your own right-of-way, but we've filled it in the way the railroads wish they might have done it.

THE INNOVATION PORTFOLIO THE RAILROADS NEEDED

The first column shows the existing train business, the core business. The second column represents the broader definition of the industry within which the core business exists—transportation, or the job trains do. The final column presents potential reciprocity businesses that use an existing right-of-way—communications. Remember that understanding your existing business is necessary to uncovering your right-of-way.

Figure 8 reveals three businesses—not just one. In this case, trains represent the core business, but this matrix also shows how investing in diesel engines is a necessary step to stay ahead of competition, though it isn't sufficient. New technologies are reinventing the ways people travel. These investments in reinvention will complement the core business but still involve moving people and things from place to place.

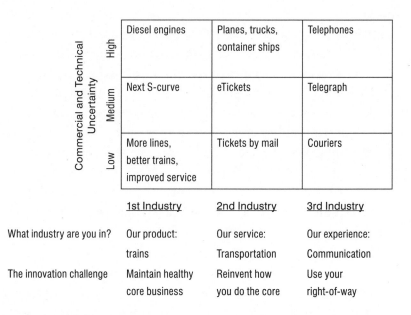

		Diesel engines	Planes, trucks, container ships	Telephones
Commercial and Technical Uncertainty	High			
	Medium	Next S-curve	eTickets	Telegraph
	Low	More lines, better trains, improved service	Tickets by mail	Couriers
		1st Industry	**2nd Industry**	**3rd Industry**
What industry are you in?		Our product: trains	Our service: Transportation	Our experience: Communication
The innovation challenge		Maintain healthy core business	Reinvent how you do the core	Use your right-of-way

Figure 8: The Innovation Portfolio the Railroads Needed.

The second problem the railroads faced was the emergence of airplanes and trucks, which moved people and freight *en masse*. When these technologies achieved maturity, they posed a direct threat to the railroads' core business. Given the funding required to re-platform and buy those diesel engines, we can only imagine the conversation that occurred, but it probably went something like this: "Strategy is about choices. We have to buy these new engines to beat our competitors. Planes are impractical and trucks are unreliable." The railroads were caught in their present reality and failed to hold aside separate innovation money to create the future.

The biggest insight from Figure 8 is that the third business for railroads could have been communications, allowing people to meet without requiring travel. With hindsight, this is easy to spot as a huge missed opportunity. The emerging technologies that would have allowed this to happen a century ago were the telegraph and, later, the telephone. The railroads had the right-of-way needed to facilitate the growth of communications, but they didn't see the potential.

As the move to a broader transportation industry occurred, all types of transportation would still need to sell trips to people and track all the things they were moving. What changed is that the new technology involved planes and trucks. The railroads maintained the rights-of-way that helped them run their trains behind the scenes, but in order to imagine themselves in the telecommunications business, they would have had to stop requiring that their customers physically board a train.

The initial move from trains to the broader definition of transportation would have been extremely expensive. They would have had to invest in new planes and airport terminals or trucks and new distribution centers. The sheer magnitude of the investment would have made it very risky, but ultimately every company must make this transition or sit on the sidelines as they become obsolete.

Smart investing can help you transition from your first industry to your second. But if you miss it, you must buy it. When e-commerce was created, it was not a matter of bricks *or* clicks—it was bricks *and* clicks. Amazon didn't have to win; retailers let them in by dismissing the importance of something that could do what they were doing with thousands of times the inventory at marginal costs that were minimal.

The right-of-way the railroads had was their literal right-of-way, the land under their tracks. Letting wires run above their tracks made it possible to communicate information. But goods still needed to be shipped and people still needed to travel. Allowing access to this right-of-way didn't meaningfully threaten the core business. To find this kind of right-of-way, you have to have an insight into the nature of your business that is more profound. Think about the *experience* behind your business.

People need to communicate, and if it is instant, they will do it ten times more frequently. You can't be on three continents in one morning, but you can make three calls. This is a huge opportunity, but nobody can do it alone. The communication business is nothing like transportation. They needed partners and the right-of-way to the railroads' land.

If you look back at the railroad portfolio matrix, you will also notice smaller business opportunities. Once you identify the new business area, look at the many low- to high-risk ways of evaluating new markets. Courier services were a very low-risk way to approach the market. Telegraphs presented a medium risk, and telephones were the riskiest of the three. The railroads needed to experiment in all these areas to create their future.

In summary, when you do apply this three-step analysis process to your own business, multiple answers will emerge. Encourage debate and create numerous maps of your future. Converge too quickly, and you might miss tremendous opportunities. Once you've uncovered your underutilized right-of-way, the next step will be searching for a partner that will enable you to accomplish what you cannot do alone.

CHAPTER 10

How to Find
the Best Partners for You

———

Businesses once grew by one of two ways: grass roots up, or by acquisition. Today they grow through alliances—all kinds of dangerous alliances. Joint ventures and customer partnerings, which, by the way, very few people understand.

PETER F. DRUCKER

———

Partnerships are hard. Don't form one unless you have to do so in order to do what you want to do—but could not do alone. Potential partners will be much easier to find in the future, but partnering will continue to be difficult.

Many corporations use the term *partnerships* too casually. Many corporations refer to themselves as partners with their customers. But most of these kinds of partnerships are really transactions, not the partnerships we are seeking in this book. Doing business with each other is not partnering; they are not creating a new business together.

To find and grow your reciprocity advantage, you have to find a partner with whom you can create a new business—a business that you could not create alone. Partnerships are very different from transactional relationships.

Transactions occur in quick succession. I give you something and you give me something of equal value back right away. Most core businesses today are built on thousands of daily transactions, or even more. Corporations used to be comfortable calling these transactions *customer-supplier relationships*. A manufacturer is the customer of a raw material supplier, for example. In turn, the manufacturer is a supplier of the store where the product will be offered for sale. And the consumer who bought the product is a customer of the store. Chains of transactions have gotten increasingly complex and global.

In a healthy business, supply-chain relationships are long-standing and stable. Out of genuine respect for each other and a desire to genuinely meet each other's needs over time, transactional customer-supplier language has fallen out of favor and has been replaced by transactional language. But in fact, these "partnerships" are usually just an extended series of transactions. The terminology of partnership has been devalued.

In a transactional relationship, each participant (even if they call each other "partners") could walk away tomorrow. In the world of price-driven transactional competition, the moment a supplier's costs get too high, the retailer's margins get too low, or the consumer's price gets too high, your partner suddenly becomes an unnecessary *supplier*, and you move on.

Everyone works to develop loyalty, and breaking up a long-term relationship with a supplier can be painful. Loyalty commands premiums in price or time before switching, but loyalty only goes so far. Ultimately, customers and suppliers do not need *you* in particular. They just need someone *like* you, who provides similar goods or services.

These relationships can be severed because the work streams between the companies are independent and separable. They come together only at the point of sale.

You should have many, many customer-supplier relationships, and these should be as respectful, warm, caring and long-lasting as possible. But as we consider developing new businesses using our right-of-way, we need to have a stricter understanding of what it means to be a partner and what it means to have a partner.

Partnerships Are Deep and Difficult

If you work for a large corporation, chances are that your company was formed as a partnership. More often than not, it was two people—Hewlett and Packard, Procter and Gamble, the Mayo brothers, Orville and Wilbur Wright, Jobs and Wozniak.

These kinds of deep partnerships are not just transactions. They brought together people with complementary skills to create a new business. These partners achieved together what they could not have accomplished alone. Because each partner brought specific proficiencies to the relationship, neither one could be easily substituted.

If your company is doing well at what it already does, you probably don't need any new partners. You've already partnered to create the business you have, and now you are running that business.

Procter and Gamble is divided into two parts—the commercial and the technical. P&G is a branded innovation company: the Procter side is running the business with all the necessary rules, and the Gamble side is product development. Karl jokes that as a product developer at P&G, he rarely related to Procter, but he was always "Gambling."

If you are to discover your reciprocity advantage and succeed in creating new reciprocity-based companies, you will bring one half of the equation to your new business. Your first challenge, however, is to understand that you aren't just looking for another person or corporation who can give you something—you need to find your missing half.

Most Partnerships Fail

We know this to be true on the commercial front and, more sadly, on the home front, where more than half of marriages in many cultures end up in divorce. Liking each other is not enough. And in the case of a business relationship, liking each other might not even be a part of the equation. While it would be *preferable* to like each other, respect and trust are far more critical. We must respect each other for what we bring to the new business.

Partners come together to do something special.

Clarity about your goals when forming a partnership is critical. You have to be able to tell your partner, "I want to do this, but I have not been able to do it until I met you." Then, each partner needs to tell the other partner *why* this is true. This is the clarity challenge.

These statements will capture the essence of the kind of partnership that is necessary to find your reciprocity advantage. You must know what you want to do, and you must realize that you could not do it alone. And you must be able to give a precise reason why you uniquely chose the other partner. Each partner must do this.

Later, when you are struggling with your partnership, you are likely to ask yourself with some remorse, What was I *thinking*? At these inevitable times, pull out these statements that brought you together and read them to reaffirm the basis of your partnership. Let everything else go.

What Right-of-Way Should You Share?

You must know your right-of-way *before* you seek a partner because that will help you understand what kind of partner you need. A core question to ask yourself is this: If I share my right-of-way away for free, will it hurt my existing business?

The concept of free is a hard one for many financial managers to grasp. Most times the answer to the question above is that it would hurt your business to share things you own. The reciprocity advantage involves sharing assets in intelligent ways *now* that will result in new growth over time.

There are times we appear to be giving assets away for free. For example, new product samples are often given away as part of a promotional trial. But the cost of the trial is factored into the product's price, so this isn't really free.

Of course, many people would like to use your right-of-way to make money that you could have made for yourself. In these cases, just say no—or charge them for the use of your right-of-way. In today's business terminology, this is *licensing*. These kinds of companies may be able to take your brand where you could not afford to—perhaps because the size of the market was too small or unprofitable for you to do on your own—but doing business with them will not fundamentally change your business. You can have good transactional relationships with these kinds of companies, but they won't make good partners.

The partnership for a reciprocity-advantage business must complement your business, not cannibalize the core business. The railroads had the land under their tracks. Allowing telegraph companies to run wires overhead did not hurt their existing business, and it did not lessen the need for trains. The telegraph business was completely separate from trains. The train people asked what seemed to them a very logical question: Would a telegram ever be as good as seeing someone in person? Unfortunately the railroads were stuck in an incrementalist's view and couldn't see the potential of communications.

The TEDx conferences did not hurt TED's existing core business of running TED conferences. TED learned that it could partner with all kinds of people and companies to create a different and complementary experience—TED benefits without doing any of the logistical work to pull off all those TEDx meetings. TED also benefits from what is to them a free talent-search process that is an inherent part of what on-the-ground TEDx organizers do.

Traditionally, partners were of similar size. Bill Hewlett and Dave Packard were individuals. Together they formed a company and essentially had equal roles in that company. William Procter and James Gamble married the Norris sisters, whose father convinced the young businessmen to work together as partners rather than compete.

In the future, the most attractive partnership opportunities will be asymmetric. Large companies may still partner with other large companies, but your new partner is likely to be an individual or a very small company who has a breakthrough technology.

It is difficult for a single person to partner directly with corporations because there are too many people in the large company who have the knowledge but not the authority to make a deal with you. For an individual to partner successfully with a big company, there must be a single point contact within the company to be the partner. That single partner needs access to the company's resources to selectively borrow what is needed but must have license to form the new company. Over-borrowing from the parent company causes the new company to simply mirror the old company, inhibiting the freedom needed to create the new business.

Partnering with millions of people around the world will become the norm for many new businesses. In these situations you will likely see key opinion leaders or early adopters, as with Microsoft's Kinect. When Kinect was first introduced, it was immediately hacked. Microsoft tried to control the hacking but quickly realized they were better off embracing the hackers and figuring out how to grow a business around them. Embracing the hackers as partners and defining their roles as value added will be critical to defining the new reciprocity advantage. This is true with the more traditional company-to-company partnerships and with a new kind of partnership that engages the lead hackers who passionately want to create a new business whether you are ready or not.

Every Partnership Should Have an Options Agreement

The new business you create will exist because you gave away your right-of-way in an intelligent way. Because you have entered a partnership in order to create something new, one of two things will happen: either the new venture will be a success, or it will disappoint. You need a plan for both possibilities.

Let's deal with disappointment first. Since the right-of-way already existed, you don't have to worry about losing money on that part of the investment. Starting new businesses using an existing right-of-way can be low risk. You read of large companies writing off large investments that are far from the core all the time. If they had used existing rights-of-way with partners, the risk would have been far more manageable.

Still, if the new business doesn't work, one of the biggest risks is that you will lose key personnel who were in that new business, which is different from the parent company. You should want to keep your original employees that were in the venture, assuming they failed *smartly*, not due to execution errors or repeating old mistakes. Smart failures can be applied to the next new business. Regardless, because this kind of learning is difficult, be prepared to lose some very good people as the true cost of doing new businesses.

Now imagine a success. Scott Anthony of Innosight—the innovation consulting firm that works with Clayton Christensen's models—tracked the growth of disruptive companies that have reached $1 billion in sales. He observed that these companies double in size every year for the first five years. So if sales in year one is $25 million, then after five years, it is $800 million. This is the billion-dollar business you are seeking. A business of this size would go for a high price and have many bidders.

The best way to buy this business is through negotiating a fair option price for purchasing the company from the beginning. You gave away the right-of-way to start the business. This is the basis for your requesting a right to participate in the success.

At the root of the railroad story, the mistake that railroad companies made was not that they missed the telecommunications revolution—who could have predicted that? Rather, they had inside information and a right-of-way that was in use. What they *missed* was negotiating partial ownership of the emerging telecommunications business.

Place your bets, but cover your options.

Each time you define a potential new business opportunity, you need to be very clear on the basis for partnership. Worksheet I summarizes the criteria from this chapter. Use it as a tool to seek and define your partnerships. When you find a potential partner, answer the questions for yourself and in the spirit of partnership, you can give them the sheet as well.

Before you complete the worksheet, recall your clarity challenge: I want to do this, but I have not been able to do it until I met you.

WORKSHEET 1: PARTNERSHIP DEFINITION

Factor	Specific Choice
What right-of-way are we sharing? What assets might we give away in order to learn how to make money in new ways?	
What is the new business we want to create with this right-of-way?	
Will this new business hurt our current business?	
Do we have commitment from top management that we want to get in this business? Who?	
Who is our single-point decision maker for this new business?	
Who will be our partner?	
Who is our partner's single-point decision maker? (There may not be one.)	
Why must we do this business with them and not someone else?	
Why must they do it with us and not someone else?	
Has our partner proven they can do what they promise to do?	
If it goes well, what option do I have to buy out the partner? If it doesn't work, can I get out?	

CHAPTER 11

How to Learn by Experimenting with Many Open Iterations

For every failure we had, we had a beautiful
spreadsheet—showing why it would work.

SCOTT COOK,
founder of Intuit

When designing experiments, big dreams matter. The experiments need to be fast and cheap, but the prize needs to be worth your trouble.

To get venture capital in Silicon Valley, you typically need to explain why your idea will earn a billion dollars per year. The world is big, so changing the world needs ideas that can be big.

In creating reciprocity advantages, we are looking for big game-changing ideas that have that billion-dollar potential.

So, what has to be true for a new idea to generate a billion dollars in annual sales? The math to create a billion-dollar business is simple:

$$\text{Price} \times \text{Quantity} = \$1 \text{ Billion}$$

The price of your offering times the quantity purchased annually equals one billion dollars. Getting the billion dollars in sales will be tough, but framing your challenge is easy.

Recall a time when one of the people in your organization came up with a new idea. He or she was excited to tell you about it but also apprehensive. Radical new ideas are fragile and need to be nurtured as they grow and develop. Inventors rightly have a tendency to be quite careful with whom they share their half-formed ideas. This equation will help deal with that fear.

Imagine an inventor approaches you with an idea. Instead of stepping back to evaluate, you step forward and say something like, "Wow, I love it. Perhaps that's our next billion-dollar business."

Likely, the inventor will be taken aback. There's almost no chance he or she has thought of that infant idea as a billion-dollar idea. Your encouragement is likely to be a positive surprise, and the most likely response will be to ask you, "What do you mean? I think it is great, but how can we make it that big?" You're now ready to work together as inventor and business manager.

Learn by Prototyping

Karl learned at P&G that many conversations about possible new businesses start with a discussion of whether or not the innovation could achieve a 20 percent premium over current offerings. If you start there, however, the conversation becomes whether you can get that or whether you will need to settle for 15 percent. Elevate the conversation by framing it around what it would take to create a billion-dollar business. This is what makes new businesses disruptive. To imagine how you might experiment to learn in search of your reciprocity advantage, you need to explore alternative ways to make money.

The simple Price $\times$ Quantity = \$1 Billion ($P \times Q = \$1B$) model allows you to look at a wide range of scenarios before stepping back to ask the important question: what would have to be true? Explore spaces that are radically different from your current business model by asking questions in which the variables are changed by orders of magnitude:

- What are you going to charge for the product or service?

- How often will it be used?

- Who is going to buy it?

- What will the cost of goods or profit margin be?

What are the answers to all these questions about your new business, and to hundreds more like them? Nobody knows. The more important insight is that you don't need to know. At this stage, just make it up!

In Table 1, the prices range from a penny per use to $10,000 per use, but all could add up to a billion-dollar business. Once the price is set, the quantity is simply the number of uses required to reach the billion-dollar sales goal. The table also shows what you would see if you were to look at the whole US market of 100 million households

TABLE 1: IMAGINING THE NEW MARKET FOR YOUR RECIPROCITY ADVANTAGE

Paths to a billion-dollar business		What habit has to be true to succeed?	
Price	Quantity	Overall market dynamics (Assume 100 million households)	Personal usage habit (Assume 10 million users)
$0.01	100 billion	It is used all the time	Many times per hour
$0.25	4 billion	100% of US households buy it weekly	Once a day
$1	1 billion	33% of US households buy it weekly	Twice per week
$10	100 million	100% of US households buy it annually	Once a month
$100	10 million	10% of US households buy it annually	Once a year
$1,000	1 million	1% of US households buy it annually	Once a decade
$10,000	100,000	0.1% of US households buy it annually	Once in a lifetime

or if you were to achieve a 10 percent market penetration, reaching 10 million individual users.

The price is there only to force the dialogue about the nature of the business you might create. By using orders of magnitudes to create the prices in the table above, we get an overall picture of market dynamics in relation to personal habits. This kind of analysis leads to two central questions:

1. What do we need to learn?
2. What kinds of experiments do we need to do to *find out* what we need to learn?

A product or service that costs twenty-five cents requires a market that includes nearly all the people in the United States or a devoted 10 percent of the population who use it daily. If you can get $1,000 per year for a product, you need reach only 1 percent of households per year. Or start by targeting ten individuals per year with a goal that everyone in the United States buys it once per decade. The nature of these businesses—represented here by various multiplication problems—would vary wildly, but they are *all* billion-dollar businesses.

To see which path you might take to create a billion-dollar business, it is helpful to consider how the habit you are asking your new users to adopt compares with their current habits. Table 2 on the next page shows examples of existing businesses and user frequency.

Place your own business in this list. Then plan to explore different models. This will help you think about how realistic it is to expect enough people to do what you are asking them to do. If you are selling consumer products, you need to be finding businesses that have consumption rates that range from once a day to once a month. If you are selling real estate or washing machines, you need to reach new customers every year, knowing that they might not be back for a decade.

Reciprocity-based businesses are likely to be built around a different, higher-frequency usage habit than your core business. The TED conference originally happened one time per year for thousands of

**TABLE 2: EXAMPLES OF BUSINESSES
WITH DIFFERENT FREQUENCY OF USAGE HABITS**

Frequency of Personal Usage	Example Businesses
Many times per hour	Google Advertising, Facebook
Once a day	Starbucks, lunch, soap
Twice per week	laundry, exercising, fast food, grocery shopping
Once a month	special dinner out, Costco, Home Depot, dry cleaning
Once a year	holiday shopping
Once a decade	moving, job search
Once in a lifetime	college, wedding

dollars. TEDx, the locally organized reciprocity-based businesses, happen hundreds of times per year, and the TED Talks online are viewed nearly continually.

Finding a business opportunity with the same frequency of usage does have the likely advantage of better fitting your current business architecture. So, it is more natural to favor these kinds of opportunities. But the risk is of limiting yourself to opportunities that are more incremental. Explore the full range of frequencies to find a long list of opportunities for growth.

Failure Is Not the Same as Risk

You must embrace creating new businesses in order to find your reciprocity advantage. But a sticking point for taking action is the belief that new businesses are very risky. New businesses do have a high failure rate, but that doesn't mean they are risky.

What do we mean when we assert that high failure rates don't necessarily mean that new businesses are risky? Imagine tossing a coin and guessing heads or tails. You will be wrong 50 percent of the time.

This is a high failure rate. But what have you risked? Nothing. This type of failure is easy and painless. But imagine I ask you to wager $10 million on a flip of the next coin. I assume you would not take this bet. Risk is the failure rate times the amount that is lost each turn. Betting $10 million with even odds is bad business.

The problem is that companies treat new business like current business. They flip too few coins and put too much money on each coin. If you know your current business well, you can safely make a few bets and go all in on those few bets. But when you move away from the core, you need to behave differently. New strategies are required for managing risk so the pain of failure is reduced.

Starting new businesses requires becoming a great risk manager.

Smaller companies or startups have an inherent risk in that they cannot afford to place many bets. They are limited in cash and resources. Most startups fail because they can afford to make only a few bets before they run out of cash. So small startups are indeed risky.

But big companies can afford to make thousands of bets to learn their way to success. Yet, big companies usually don't succeed either. Why?

Many big companies place too much money on each bet. They need to find ways to construct and manage incredibly small bets. In this chapter and the next we show how to construct better bets.

Think again about the coin toss example above. Each time you flip a coin, you have a 50-percent chance of failure. So you will guess right about half the time. You will also fail half the time. If it doesn't cost you anything to play this coin-flipping game, how risky is it? While this game has an unacceptably high failure rate for a business, it has zero risk. It might be boring, but you could play the game all day.

But if each turn costs you a million dollars, will you still play? No. What changed? We added a risk—a million dollars per toss. This is an unacceptable level of risk. Yet most new business efforts place all their money on one big bet. "Go big or go home" is a recipe for going home.

To win the new business game you need a new approach to risk management.

Writing Options on Your Future

Most people who buy stock in a company expect that company to continue doing what it has been doing, and therefore plan on returns similar to past returns.

Investing in a company's stock is very similar to investing in innovating your core business. There is a long history of what worked and what didn't, plus a narrow range of returns. An extension of the base business has limited downside risk but also limited upside potential. This model puts large teams of people on a project from the beginning, pulls out the best practices that were used last time, and hopes for the best. Not everything works; investment in a current business is inherently low risk and has a low rate of failure.

This creates a culture of expectations for success. When the cash flow is known, companies can use traditional tools such as net present value (NPV) to accurately assess a business's potential.

The problem is we don't know whether a new business will be successful or not. The further you venture from the core of your current business, the less you know. This creates a bimodal situation. If you are right, you make a lot of money. If you are wrong, you lose a lot of money. It's our coin toss dilemma but with money attached to it.

The tool you need for managing high risk is an *option*. An option is a specific right to buy something of value at a predetermined price at a particular time in the future for a specific cost today. Options trading can get very complicated, but you need to understand only the basic concept to create innovation investments for the future.

An option is a specific right to buy something of value at a predetermined price at a predetermined time in the future for a specific cost today. Let's say you have the option to buy a stock at $95 per share in 60 days for a stock that is trading at $90 today. You might pay $0.50 per share for this privilege. If in 60 days the stock is selling for $105, you get to buy it for $95 and immediately sell it at $105, pocketing the difference of $10 per share. Congratulations, you win. On the other hand, if the stock went down to $85 per share, you would not buy the stock. Rather, you would let your option expire, losing your $0.50

per share. So you could make $10 on your $0.50 investment or lose your $0.50. The potential gain is 2,000 percent, while the most you could lose is 100 percent. If you had owned the same stock, your gain would have been 17 percent, or your loss would have been 5 percent. Options are placed to make your money go further when there are large unknowns.

Don't worry about the math. The key options concepts here are these:

1. You pay a very small percentage of the cost. So, you can invest in many possible projects.
2. Options expire. They don't have a life of their own, unlike stale development projects that never seem to die.
3. The risk is limited to the initial investment. Every 60 days you can walk away or reinvest.

The common error is to create a big team and spend a million dollars and one year on one idea. An options approach takes that budget and cuts it into small chunks. Teams of one to three people work for 30–60 days and come back to the senior management group with proposals for the next 30–60 days and how they would spend the next small chunk. This approach by learning will explore up to twenty times the number of opportunities. As with the uncertain stock market, many small bets to find the winner are better than one single investment.

Find the Killer Issues

Consider Scott Cook's beautiful spreadsheet problem that opened this chapter. The level of detail in a current business model is extreme. Why? We know so much about the current business that a spreadsheet is a great tool. The problem with applying that tool to a new business is that it requires adding assumptions upon assumptions. The result will look great but have no meaning.

Clayton Christensen's consulting company Innosight, led by Scott Anthony and Mark Johnson, has a series of great tools for exposing and possibly reconsidering the 100 assumptions you are making when building a new business.[43] This is a wonderful exercise in humility. You and your team will quickly find out just how much you don't know.

Your list of assumptions can be divided into two piles: the ones that would make no difference if you were wrong and the ones that would kill your business if you were wrong. If it won't kill you, document your best guess for future use. If it *would* kill you, start assessing your options.

Experiment with the killer issues. This is where you need to learn the most. Many exploratory teams tend to work on the stuff they know how to do. Marketing people work on the brand positioning. Scientists work on finding the new molecule. Finance people make spreadsheets and calculate NPVs. We all do what comes naturally, but that doesn't reduce the risk unless it is a killer issue. When trying to find your reciprocity advantage in a new business space, you need to learn by experimenting—again and again and again.

BUY OPTIONS ON THE TOP TWO KILLER ISSUES FOR THE NEXT 60 DAYS

For a business to be successful, two things are obvious:

1. Someone has to want to buy what you are selling.
2. There has to be a reason they will pay you.

The first issue is your commercial risk. The second issue is your technical risk. The best way to reduce risk is to work on each of these risks at the same time for the next 60 days to see if you can find a way to solve them. Until you can crack the toughest issues between you and success, working on anything else is a waste of money.

But this is counterintuitive because most people want to work on what they already know how to do. Many may be thinking, If they find the answer to that question, then I'll be behind in getting my work done. So, I better do my usual work too.

It is true that you will have to eventually figure out the brand name and the consumer positioning and the supply stream. But if the killer issues are not resolved first, you won't need a brand name at all. Invention work is done better in quick succession. Production work is best done in parallel. New business is invention, not production.

Focus on your learning as inexpensive options on your new business. A helpful rule of thumb helps with planning the options. If the size of the prize is $100 million is sales, a good option costs 1 percent or $1 million. You would gladly pay $1 million to make $100 million. So, the total budget for finding a $100-million idea would be $1 million. But you are not going to be right the first time. So break that $1 million into ten bets of $100,000 each.

Rather than running a single million-dollar project for a year, have your team run ten $100,000 projects sequentially for a year. Spend that money by giving the team $100,000 to run the first project for 30 days. This is an "option" that you can then renew in 30 days by giving them the next $100,000 to continue the learning or let that option expire and fund a new, different option based on the learning. Dividing the funding and time up into small increments focuses the organization on fast, agile learning. This is a series of quick looks at managing the top two killer issues, which is the key to nurturing breakthrough ideas.

Thousands of Prototypes

What do your teams do during the 30–60 days you gave them for learning? They prototype their ideas to see if they can solve the killer issues. Solving those issues will allow them to tackle the next ones. Eventually failing to solve the issues will be the equivalent of expired options.

How many prototypes did you make last month? How many did your organization make overall last month? What did the last prototype look like when it was shown to you? How much did that prototype cost to make? How many were shown to you in the last presentation? How much time does it take to revise a prototype?

To win at creating new businesses that are different from what you already do—new businesses that may reshape an industry or create a new one—you need to efficiently make and evaluate hundreds, or even thousands, of prototypes per month. This means you have to be able to make dozens each day. So these prototypes must be extremely cheap, much less than $10 each. These are probably very different from what is being created by your team today. So that last single winning design nicely painted and accompanied by a 100-slide Power-Point won't get you there.

Resolving killer issues requires rapid, cheap prototyping. This kind of options work requires a work process developed by David Kelley called *design thinking*. Kelley is one of the founders of IDEO, a top design firm that has been honored for a wide range of products and services in health care, business, finance, education, and non-profits. Kelley sees design thinking as a way to transform business. He recently founded a design school at Stanford. Just a short walk from IDEO's headquarters in Palo Alto, the d.school is a collaboration between Stanford's school of mechanical engineering and their graduate school in business. Once an experiment, it is now the hottest class on campus regardless of what discipline you are studying.

To help you get started, IDEO is sharing its right-of-way—design thinking—with the world to shape the next generation of leaders who will need to think like designers. This summarizes the steps to design thinking:

ESSENTIAL STEPS IN DESIGN THINKING

1. **Frame the challenge**—What killer issue do you want to resolve?
2. **Brainstorm the issue**—Create at least 100 ideas to address the issue.
3. **Assimilate**—Choose 2–3 ideas to prototype.
4. **Prototype solutions**—Create crude models.
5. **Share the models with potential users**—Get feedback using your crude model.
6. **Refine prototypes to reflect input**—Make it better.
7. **Share the refined prototypes again**—Stay crude.
8. **Share your range of prototypes with management**—Get their builds.[44]

Initial sessions take only a day or two. The overall process for IDEO takes twelve weeks from start to finish. If you are in the d.school, your grade depends on having a new business defined and proposed in that time.

Karl was a judge in a final competition where teams pitched their ideas. Each judge decided whether or not to "fund" a proposal. The top grade went to the team with the most votes to fund, and the lowest grade went to the team with the fewest votes.

Cracking tough problems means rapid learning. Most cultures are high performance, not high learning. A successful growth company needs both cultures and the systems to support both.

Using your right-of-way to build a big business starts with imagining what has to be true to build a big business. By starting with identifying what has to be true to have your idea be big, you can focus on the barriers to achieving that huge success. Working from the future backward, we identify the key constraints, or "killer issues," that must be addressed to make the project worth doing. It can take thousands of iterations to create a blockbuster new business. Rapid prototyping makes this affordable and fast. Most companies will need to build this skill.

The solution to starting new reciprocity businesses is using options thinking and rapid prototyping. Make to learn, not make to sell.

Learning by experimenting is necessary to create reciprocity-based businesses with low risk. Having identified the right-of-way from analyzing your current business, you need to efficiently experiment to create the prototypes of the future businesses.

AN EXAMPLE OF THE STEPS
FOR PROTOTYPING A NEW BUSINESS

- Define the size of the prize: $P \times Q = \$1B$ global market. Inside a large company, $100 million in incremental sales is usually considered large enough. Aim higher at the beginning to truly find something worth doing. Find what has to be true to hit a billion dollars.

- Assign one or two A-team people to work on this project, ideally one from inside the company and one from outside. Junior people working in high-risk areas will fail. If this is the future of the company, staff it with the leader.

- Set learning goals and a budget for the next year. For $100-million ideas, the total budget would be $1 million, or 1 percent of the size of the prize. One of the biggest mistakes is spending $10 million to make $10 million.

- Determine the two biggest risks. Then design experiments to learn about just these two risks over the next 60 days, spending no more than 10 percent of the budget. This will force the team to focus and use cheap prototypes.

- Based on what is learned, either continue to work on these risks by giving them another 10 percent of the budget and 60 more days, or, having mastered them, choose the next two biggest risks to work on.

- Keep learning and scale the winner. When progress becomes stagnant, stop work and let the option expire. The 60-day time frame keeps the team focused and learning. If there is still no progress, move on. If you crack it, go big.

The good news is that the process of design thinking is well documented, and there are lots of people who can help you learn how to do it. The tougher news is that senior leadership will need to get on board if it is going to work.

Building the culture to do this is hard work when your day-to-day business is not done this way. This is why partnering can be a path to success. Choose partners that have this complementary approach as the way they work, and then follow them.

Your New Reciprocity Advantage Business Plan

At the beginning of this chapter we discussed how users of your reciprocity-based businesses are unlikely to have the same usage habits as those who use your existing business. Enabling these habit changes will require new business models, and those models will drive the killer issues. So finding the underlying factors for creating a new billion-dollar business starts with imagining what has to be true to create a billion-dollar market. This is the P×Q=$1B exercise.

This exercise gives you a clearer understanding of your current business by asking you to capture its pricing and usage dynamics. Then to create the new business, imagine those levels of consumption at 100 times higher and then 100 times lower.

This is not an exercise that you run once. The goal is to get you started down the path of imagining the whole range of possible businesses. Keep the discussion going until you find something that you're passionate about—*if* you could just resolve these killer issues.

Step 1: Write down your assumptions for the current business, as well as the radically faster and slower consumption habits you've chosen to model. This will help align you and your team to the nature of the proposed new business that will exploit your right-of-way.

Step 2: Figure out what are the really risky unknowns and focus on the biggest ones. These are your killer issues. If you can't find answers to these, you won't succeed.

Worksheet 2 will help you find your best scale.

TABLE 2: LEARNING BY EXPERIMENTING—
HOW TO FIND YOUR BEST SCALE

	Step 1: Answer the questions.	Step 2: Which answers do you doubt are true?
Define your current business model.		
What is your largest user group?		
What is the price per use?		
What is the usage frequency?		
Imagine the new business offering is used 100 times more frequently than current business offerings.		
Describe the new usage pattern. When would your product or service be used?		
Who would use it this frequently?		
What would the price have to be for this to generate a billion dollars in annual sales?		
Who could afford to buy it at this price?		
Does technology exist to allow this usage?		
Does technology exist to make this product at this cost per use?		
Imagine the new business offering is used 100 times less often than your current business offerings.		
Describe the new usage pattern. When would your product or service be used?		
Who could use it this frequently?		
What would the price have to be for this to generate a billion dollars in annual sales?		
Who could afford to buy it at this price?		
Does technology exist to allow this usage?		
Does technology exist to make this at this cost per use?		

CHAPTER 12

How to Scale
Your Reciprocity Advantage

If it isn't scalable, it isn't worth doing.

VINOD KHOSLA,
Sun Microsystems founder
and green venture capitalist

Creating your reciprocity advantage will allow you to make a big difference for a long time. *Scalable* reciprocity, however, will require designing for scalability from the beginning. This chapter shows you how to design for scale. Reciprocity is good, but massively scalable reciprocity is growth that reshapes industries.

You will know your reciprocity advantage is ready to scale when your service or product meets three criteria—it's desirable, viable, and ownable.

Failing to meet all three criteria will severely limit or even doom your reciprocity advantage.

As we discussed in Chapter 11, the reason experimenting to learn is such a critical skill is that new business ideas are rarely desirable, viable, *and* ownable from the start. Ideas need to be nurtured to solve for the missing pieces of the puzzle. Before you can successfully scale, you need partners who have the missing skills for this new business and you will need to have a culture of rapid prototyping.

Start with something that has two out of three of the criteria: you

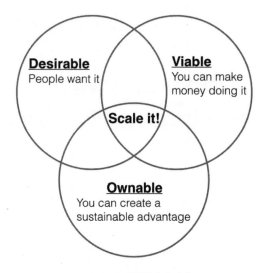

Figure 9: DVO Model.

know people desire it and you know the viable business model—you just need to make it ownable. Or you could start with an ownable technology and a viable business model, and then work to find something desirable that can be made. Two out of three is easy. When you have all three—desirable, viable, and ownable—you will be ready to scale rapidly.

Is It Desirable?

No one ever asked for an iPod before they saw one. But that's not an excuse for pretending that success can't be *seen* in advance.

You can't just ask people what they want. However, you can observe. The tensions and frustrations that call out for new products are observable if you spend time with people rather in the office or behind the mirror in focus groups. You can be with them while they are living their lives and ask lots of questions. You can inquire about hopes and fears. You can listen for the future. To be a truly desirable product, service, or experience, it will need to provide a transformational benefit.

Is your idea transformational?

Its users must be able to say that it is different in *kind*, not just incrementally better. Most companies simply are not objective enough to see if a new product is transformational or not. In order to attract a large investment, there is a tendency to oversell the benefit as *transformational* just to get the project approved.

Swiffer was transformational. As the product was being prototyped, a mother told Karl, "I have exactly four minutes between the time I put my child down until I have to go back to her. If I tried to get the vacuum out or fill a bucket with water, by the time I got the vacuum out, the time would be up or the water would get cold before I could use it."

Using Swiffer to clean has no start-up time. It takes cleaning from a process that must be done continuously in a big block of time to one that can be done in short blocks of time (four minutes or less). Swiffer is to cleaning what the early Blackberry was to checking email away from your desk. Swiffer doesn't clean better; it cleans *differently*. As a result, that mom could do her cleaning in small chunks of time, and her house was cleaner than ever before. The benefit was transformational, but it was not obvious until after she did it.

Is your idea intuitive?

Intuition is what sets Apple products apart from its competitors. Apple products are beautiful. And ever since the creation of the mouse, they are also intuitive for most people—unless they grew up using PCs.

All Apple products have the same language of swipes and pinches, regardless of the app or the device. You never saw a swipe before you swiped, but once you saw it, you got it right away. Why? Swiping is something you already do when you change pages in a book. It is intuitive.

Both Bob and Karl had a range of experiences with Douglas C. Engelbart, the inventor of the mouse and many other key ideas that we take for granted as part of our digital life. Go online and search for the "mother of all demos." You'll recognize the future he was talking about in 1968, while he was at what was then called the Stanford Research Institute. When Karl met with Doug, he asked him one question: "Is there anything else you wanted to do, but no one would listen to you?" He politely chuckled and said, "Nobody will take more than five to ten minutes to learn anything. Too many people are working on creating new technology, and not enough people are working on making existing technology usable."

When Steve Jobs saw the Engelbart mouse, it had five buttons on it. Jobs didn't want any buttons—he wanted people to know how to use it just by looking at it. Engelbart imagined that his system (originally called NLS) would have as many commands as there are words in the English language. If we could have learned all those commands, we would indeed have augmented the human intellect in ways that Engelbart had hoped. Instead, we must strive for innovations that are simple yet powerful—simple but not simplistic.

Being transformational and intuitive are at odds with each other. This dilemma-ridden space, however, is the space where breakthroughs can occur. The more transformational the idea is, the less intuitive it is likely to be. Conversely, the more intuitive it is, the more likely it has only incremental benefit—not transformational.

The lesson: start by finding a transformational benefit, and then stick with it until you can figure out how to make it intuitive. Have great clarity about the transformational benefit but great flexibility about how you might get there.

Mr. Clean Magic Eraser is able to remove black marks from walls with only water and the eraser. Many black marks can't be removed even with strong cleaners, but Mr. Clean Magic Eraser can do it. To the user, it seems like magic.

The product is made of a foam that turns into a mild abrasive slurry when wet. As you rub, you peel the dirt off the wall but leave the paint intact. Karl's product development team originally called the product Mr. Clean Sponge since people already clean with sponges. But the product prototype, unlike a typical sponge, had a tendency to pill up and fall apart when used. The prototype users loved the product but were confused at what they perceived as the lack of durability. They asked us to make it more durable.

At P&G, Karl's team considered the possibilities. Making it more durable didn't seem possible and wasn't key to its cleaning performance anyway. The breakthrough was visualizing the process of removing a black mark from a white surface. Where have you seen that before? When you make a mistake with a pencil on paper, you erase the error. It was an apt analogy for erasing black marks off a white wall—and everybody could relate to it. Mr. Clean Sponge became the Magic Eraser. That framing made the product desirable *and* intuitive.

To be truly desirable on a large scale, your reciprocity advantage must be both transformational and intuitive. Then, once you have the product, you must figure out how to bring it to life as a business.

Is It Viable?

Viability is about the business model. If people desire a new product and the manufacturing people can make it, but you can't make enough money at that price, you don't have a scalable solution. Reciprocity is not philanthropy. Reciprocity-advantage businesses like Smarter Planet, for example, are profitable. If you subsidize a new business, it is very likely to die when you remove the support. There are stories about Silicon Valley billionaires who failed time and again before their eventual success. Some people think this means that failure is not important to entrepreneurs and that they take failure well. We have yet to meet a successful entrepreneur who liked failing.

So, what's the truth behind the failure mystique? Successful entrepreneurs fail *smartly*. They may have failed ten times before their big success, but each failure was a very small financial loss. No one loses $100 million of someone else's money and gets a second chance. Successful entrepreneurs lose a little money and learn. This is the essence of rapid prototyping. A viable new business has two components: it's affordable and structurally attractive.

1. How much will you charge for your product?

2. Is it affordable for the people you want to use it?

In Chapter 11 we looked at several business models for making a billion dollars. In general, the more frequently you use a product, the less you can afford to pay for each use. Each business has a pricing range. What's yours?

In consumer goods, the number of people you can expect to try a product is well correlated with specific price points. The market for $100 appliances in US households is about 1 percent per year. At $10 per unit, you can expect about 10 percent to try it in a year. For a purchase price below $5, you might get 20 percent to buy it on impulse and figure it out later. If you are in Europe, replace the five dollars with five euros or five pounds, and the relationship holds. Similarly, in Japan about 700 yen will work. These are more expensive than $5, but these are the high-volume price-point equivalents for the different markets.

In developing markets, income distribution makes this calculation more complicated. The relationships are equivalent, but they have more dire overtones. It is common to refer to $0.10 as the cost of an egg. So, would the person prefer to use your product or buy an egg?

In all cases, your product needs to fit within an existing budget. To buy your product, what would people give up?

Consider these rules of thumb when you're calculating the real odds of creating a major new market, and size your business accordingly. Don't bet that you will be the one to break the rules. Large markets tend to take a decade to develop and have a steady growth curve equal to the annual trial potential based on the price you charge.

Do you know what is affordable for your idea?

The business structure for your reciprocity advantage will be very important as well. The popular wisdom is that you can give away the razors and make money on the blades, but this structure rarely works out. First of all, a better description of the current razor business model is to make money on the razors and make *a ton* of money on the blades. Second, shaving is an established habit, so the economics of trial are well known and can be treated as investments. The next improvement in razors is not likely to be transformational, no matter how much better they are, because it will still be the same task at the same time of day by the same people who would otherwise shave with their current blade. Applying this model to a new business will bankrupt you.

New businesses have unknown frequencies of usage. If you give away the product, you will encounter two problems. Most people who are given something free will take it. They will have no motivation, however, to work the product into their daily routine. Most free samples for products requiring a habit change are simply not used.

Even if someone uses a free sample, you can't predict the frequency of use. The repurchase cycle is unknown, and unknowns lead to uncertain cash flows. And for a new business to succeed, cash is king.

The solution is simple: price your product or service to pay out the cost of a trial. You don't have to get the original investment recovered right away, but you must cover the cost of the trial.

In practice, this means charging a higher-than-desired price to start the market and then lowering the price, as the repeat cycle becomes known. The secret to success is staying at breakeven until the cash flow is known.

If you know you will reduce the price in a year by implementing known cost savings that would occur even if you did not grow, it is fair to include these savings in your structural economics from the start. A common fault is to confuse those savings that come from the product or service cost savings with the economics of scale. Until you have scale, it is risky to count on those savings.

What are the breakeven economics for your idea?

This is your structural cost for the new business. If your reciprocity advantage is both affordable and structurally attractive, it is likely to be viable.

The higher you price, the smaller your initial market size will be, but your structural economics will be better. Breakthroughs occur when you have something that is affordable and structurally attractive.

Fast, low-cost learning is the secret to winning. If you must be first, the idea must be small. Be the fastest learner.

Have you planned a price that is affordable?

And do you have the cost structure that matches that price?

Is It Ownable?

One of the first questions any investor will ask is this: "Is it patentable?" Patents are great things. They give you exclusive rights for up to twenty years. The problem is that the patent world is extremely crowded, so getting patents is a slow, costly, and uncertain process. More important, patents offer far less protection than many investors think. It may be possible for your reciprocity advantage to be ownable in important ways without being patentable.

Consider the current mess in the smart phone industry. A truly game-changing patent is bound to be infringed upon by competition. Years later, if you win a court settlement, your payment will be a fraction of the profit made by the competitor who infringed on your patent.

The best patents give you a valuable head start to develop a new business. Get your patents, but develop a strategy for owning a piece of the market in five years, when the market is big enough to care about.

There are two components to ownability: feasibility and proprietary position.

Is it feasible for you to make it?

It seems self-evident that you have to know how to make your new business's product or offer the service. The inventors have shown you a beautiful demo of the transformation that they have made possible. So, is it feasible?

For an invention to be declared feasible, it needs to be able to be done at the scale at which you intend to run your business. As the invention progresses from paper to lab to pilot plant to plant to global expansion, it gets reinvented at each point.

This is why you need to estimate the size of the market early. You may create or buy an invention that works in the lab, but that invention might never work at full scale, in which case you have a nice patent on a worthless invention. Most inventions never get tried out. They may have solved a problem, but they never had the cost structure or ability to scale. Many partnerships will fail because what the invention originally promised to deliver at a particular level of performance and at a specific cost cannot be achieved.

When something is first invented, you do not have to know immediately how to scale it. Rather, you need to pull together the right group of people to assess the development potential and have a firm plan for managing the risk. If it fails to scale, you will have to find a new invention. This can be a major issue if you have partnered around that invention. This is why you often need to have many partnerships.

Do you know if your idea can be feasible at the required scale?

Imagine you had no patents. How would you win?

Once people saw the first iPhone, all other phones were just phones. Swiffer caused people to rethink the very idea of quick cleaning. All video talks are now compared to TED Talks. All of these are powerful archetypes, and that didn't happen by accident. Carefully crafted, iPhone, Swiffer, and TED all have ownable territory in their marketplaces.

Your proprietary position is the sum total of what it takes to win versus the likely competitors. Venture capitalists often hate this idea. It is so much simpler to believe you will have a killer patent. In practice, the best ways to have a strong proprietary position are not technical.

The Food and Drug Administration (FDA) is a huge source of competitive advantage. They grant exclusive licenses to drug and device manufacturers—regardless of the patents—based on the clinical study data that show safety and effectiveness. Mucinex is an excellent example of a brand that used an old technology with a new data set to get exclusivity. The active ingredient (guaifenesin) is one of the older cough remedies. Adams, the maker of Mucinex, created new data on benefits related to phlegm buildup and built a huge new brand that was sold to Reckitt Benckiser for a healthy profit.

Sales-channel exclusivity is a very common source of proprietary position. The incumbent brands have what is referred to as *real estate,* which they control in the grocery stores. Similarly, software companies have relationships with your IT department that give them a strong ownership position. Having a better, patented idea is not a guarantee of a strong proprietary position.

Ultimately the relationship you have with existing people is the beginning of your proprietary position. This is in part why leveraging existing right-of-way is so powerful.

What is the source of your sustainable competitive position, even if you cannot legally own it?

Make sure your inventions can scale—otherwise, they aren't inventions you need. Too many companies invest quickly to build production capacity and then find the invention doesn't work. Invest in those experiments that show whether scaling is possible.

Then focus on building a strong proprietary position using all the tools you can. Take full advantage of the transformative nature of your new business to create the new archetype for the category you are creating.

There is an overemphasis on patents that get in the way of building the business. When companies buy businesses from an entrepreneur, they pay a percentage of sales for a technology patent and a multiple of sales for a brand. Build something that is worth a multiple of sales, not a small percentage of sales.

Do you know your feasibility at scale?

Do you have a clear plan for building your ownable position?

Fast, cheap prototyping is the key to finding success. We discussed how to do this in Chapter 11. In this chapter we highlight the criteria for finding success. Winning business models will feature products that are desirable, viable, *and* ownable—all three. Having only two of the three is not sufficient.

Your Reciprocity Advantage Score Card

Use the following Reciprocity Advantage Score Card to score your reciprocity advantage idea. Your goal is to score a 6 out of 6. When you start, your new idea will not score a 6. You will need to cycle through finding your right-of-way, finding the best partner, and experimenting to learn many times before you will be ready to scale.

The best way to use this tool is to have a small team discussion with no more than five people. We prefer using forced choice: "Yes, definitely" or "No, we don't think so." Inevitably teams like to also use 0.5 for "Well, maybe." You can temporarily allow this, but those *maybes* are signs of where you need to do more work—after you address the factors that scored "No."

Why do you need a 6 out of 6? Only a small number of missing links can be managed when you are in market, and then, only as long as you are aware of the risk. A 5 rating is a passable score if you have a great risk-mitigation plan in hand. Anything less, and the innovation will look like the children's game *Whack-a-Mole*, where problems are popping up everywhere. Just when you think you are in control, another problem pops up. There never seems to be enough time to do it right from the beginning, but there's always enough time to fix it.

Our advice is not to expand if you score 4 or below. Keep experimenting.

Scale It

When you finally get that score of 6, stop prototyping and run as fast as you can.

Your team now has a viable business model and a plan. While this is still a new business to the users who will be buying your product or service, you have deep understanding and a solid success model.

The difference between a new business and an existing business is what Scott Anthony of Innosight calls the "knowledge-to-assumption ratio." In an existing business you have lots of knowledge and few assumptions—it can continue to do what you have already found successful. This has low risk and probably has a low return since it

RECIPROCITY ADVANTAGE SCORE CARD—
ARE YOU READY TO SCALE?

Factor	Criteria	Yes=1 No=0	Your rationale
Transformational	Does the product deliver against a significant, unmet need—with no alternatives? (There should not be alternate solutions.)		
Intuitive	Do people get it? Do they immediately know what to do with it? (Complicated communication can be deadly.)		
Affordable	Is it affordably priced relative to high-volume benchmark categories? (Affordability varies by target customer.)		
Structurally attractive	Can you afford a trial and get to target margin in two years? (Even trials should be profitable. The razors-and-blades model rarely works for new entries.)		
Feasible	Do you know if the inventions will scale to the size of your desired market? (You don't get a second chance on capital investment. Know before you buy.)		
Proprietary position	Is there a whole-brand strategy, including consumer-preferred design and trademarks and commercial relationships alongside utility patents? (Be a big player when the market develops.)		
Total	**6 of 6 is ready to go** **5 of 6 is marginal** **4 or less will fail**		

is not very different from the market as a whole. However, having prototyped your way through killer issues, you no longer have little knowledge and lots of assumptions. Your experiments have replaced those assumptions with new knowledge.

When you know your product is desirable, you know you have a viable financial model, and you know how to sustain the business long enough to get a return, you have created a low-risk, high-potential business. You now have a knowledge-to-assumption ratio that is as good as an existing business.

When that happens, scale it! Execution quality still counts, so be just as vigilant in going to market, but implement your plan.

The main reason new businesses fail is that they scale before having all the needed answers. A second reason new businesses fail, however, is that they fail to go all in when they have a clear path to success. When your reciprocity advantage meets all three criteria—it's desirable, viable, and ownable—you have a winning idea. Speed is now on your side. Run!

Knowing When to Quit

Finally, not everything will work. You will need agility to read and react quickly to whatever happens. A common challenge is that companies are less agile when it comes to stopping a bad project.

How do you know if it is time to go home? In his experience, Karl has found only two things that always correlate with success for a disruptive new business idea: passion and keeping commitments.

Only people with passion will change the world. If after trying something for a period of time, you or your team loses passion for it, stop doing it.

Passionate people don't always change the world, of course. Passion *can* create blindness, but passionate people may also see a possibility that you don't. If we make a passionate team move at the speed of our ability to understand them, they may be too late. You don't have to understand their passion to help nurture their idea. This, however, will require faith in concert with measurement.

Ask the team to give you a milestone for the next 60 days. Write it down. Then 60 days later, have team members compare what they accomplished versus what they thought they would accomplish. If they meet or exceed the goal, get another milestone and step back. If they miss the milestone, have them give you another commitment for the next 60 days.

If after 180 days they are still not hitting their milestones, smart teams often lose their passion. Stop the project if you see no passion. If, however, after 180 days they are missing their milestones but they are still passionate, there may be hope. The problem may not be that they were wrong. Rather, they could have underestimated the size of the problem. Don't let them keep doing the same thing. Get them outside help to create a new plan perhaps, but don't give up.

Once they look at the new plan, they may decide it is too hard. They may even ask you to stop it. Or, you could start the 60-day milestones again. This iterative, team-led milestone process is the best way to get a breakthrough. Most new businesses can make a huge amount of progress in less than a year. That's because ultimately a year is a long time taken in 60-day learning increments. Be disciplined.

Luck is part of what it will take to be successful, but discipline will help you be lucky more often.

CHAPTER 13

When the Future Is Reciprocity

———

Takers have a distinctive signature: they like to get
more than they give . . . in the workplace, givers are a
relatively rare breed. They tilt reciprocity in the other
direction, preferring to give more than they get.

ADAM GRANT,
Give and Take

———

The popularity of Adam Grant's wonderful 2013 book *Give and Take*
reinforces the notion that giving can contribute to business success
over time. Grant distinguishes between *givers* and *takers* and draws an
explicit link to reciprocity. We are focused in *The Reciprocity Advantage*
on organizational reciprocity, but Adam Grant has provided a gift to
us all by documenting the lessons of personal reciprocity advantage.

Give and Take is doing much to encourage individual leaders to consider the advantages of reciprocity for their own personal long-term
growth. Being a giver in Grant's sense will help you find your own
personal reciprocity advantage, even if you end up giving more than
you get in the short run. It will also fuel efforts to find your corporate
reciprocity advantage, which is our focus in this book. We believe that
givers will be much better at creating reciprocity advantage for their
companies and for themselves.

Neuroscience and the psychology of happiness are teaching us
that the happy people are those who give, the happiest are those who
learn how to forgive, and the least happy are those who carry grudges.

Reciprocity advantage will be fueled by this basic insight into human motivation. Interestingly, most of the world religions teach the value of giving, but now neuroscience and the psychology of happiness are teaching us the same principles—backed up by data. A new appreciation for the value of giving will fuel new models for reciprocity advantage.

This is our wrap-up chapter, where we focus on answering two core questions:

- How do you apply reciprocity-advantage logic to yourself?
- What tools and resources can help you now?

We are convinced that the future will be shaped by reciprocity. There are many things you can do right now, however, that will make this future both possible and practical.

Reciprocity Advantage for Yourself

Bob was leading a workshop for top leaders at a major retailer while we were in the early stages of writing this book. After he introduced the VUCA World and gave a taste of the latest IFTF ten-year forecast, one of the workshop participants raised her hand. "I'm not prepared for this future," she said. "I have no idea where I will fit. What do I do now?"

The workshop participant who said she was not prepared was one of the most impressive people in this very impressive class of rising stars. Everyone froze on her words and immediately jumped to her support. She was expressing something that they were all feeling.

Her colleagues were amazed that she was courageous enough to voice such stark fears in front of her peers, with whom she was already competing for top jobs. None of them—all top leaders for a great company—felt prepared for this future. The future they had been anticipating had been cancelled.

Right then, Bob had one of those moments in front of a group when he didn't know how to respond. He had frightened them about the VUCA World and all its threats. But he had not empowered them to win in this future world. They felt stuck.

Bob quickly thought back to his many discussions with Karl about the four steps to reciprocity advantage. If these four steps helped corporations make sense of the VUCA World, why couldn't they work for this bright rising star?

He started with her concerns and began engaging with her. He looked directly at her and asked four questions to help her decide what to do.

The first question was inspired by the first step toward finding your reciprocity advantage but rephrased as a personal question:

What is your personal right-of-way?

In other words, he asked her to list her strengths, strengths that she might be underutilizing, strengths that would serve her well in the VUCA World of the future.

Her colleagues jumped in and helped her answer this question, and she had many strengths. Since she had just read *Leaders Make the Future*, Bob reminded her that this is a test of the future leadership skill called Clarity. The best leaders in the VUCA World are very clear about where they are going but very flexible about how they get there. A rich conversation ensued.

Then, he asked a second question:

What new partners might allow you to do things you could not do alone, to develop and expand your personal right-of-way?

This included the people in the room but also friends, family—and people she didn't even know yet. Who might she learn from who is more familiar with the elements of the VUCA World that she finds most disturbing?

It turned out that she had staff members on her team who were half her age. She also had a brother that was much younger than her. Bob suggested cross-generational mentoring so that she could learn from her staff and her younger brother. She was already a mentor to many, but the VUCA World requires us all to be mentored by each other.

Several months later she reported that these suggestions turned out to be effective. She realized that she had been doing too much "coaching" and even a bit of "preaching" about what she thought others should do, but what she needed to do was more *listening*. She obviously had a lot of wisdom and leadership to offer, but she needed to step back and figure out how to partner with new people in new ways. Once she realized this and accepted the VUCA World of her work, she felt calmer and more focused. She even said that she'd developed a sense of "weird comfort" about all the uncertainty around her.

Her colleagues in the room had also volunteered to partner with her. They were beginning to model the leadership skill that Silicon Valley visionary Howard Rheingold first called Smart Mob Organizing, which is finding the best partners and organizing them to help you, making good choices about which medium is good for what task.[45]

Bob's third question was

What experiments could you do to learn how to expand your own right-of-way, by working with partners?

How could she get lots of personal experiments going quickly, on the assumption that she needs to fail early, fail often, and fail cheaply in order to learn how to move ahead as a leader?

What is required here is Immersive Learning Ability, which would allow her to dive into worlds that she needs to learn about—even if they make her uncomfortable. She will also need to practice Rapid Prototyping, which will allow her to fail early, often, and cheaply in order to succeed in the long term.

And his last question was

How could you scale your own right-of-way to maximize your impact?

This was a question of personal scaling. In regards to her career path, how will she have the greatest impact—given the external future forces of the next decade and given her own strengths and weaknesses?

Responding to this question requires the most sophisticated future leadership skill—Commons Creating. This is the ability to build shared assets that offer value to you—but also to others. Bob also suggested that she think about her leadership legacy. Columbia Business

School professor Bill Klepper, for example, has a wonderful approach to helping leaders develop their own personal leadership credo, what we would refer to as your personal right-of-way and your reciprocity advantage.[46]

Bob encouraged this rising-star leader to engage with the future instead of being overwhelmed by it. That is the challenge that we all face. We know that the VUCA World is frightening, but we also know that what wins in this world is great clarity about where we are going—combined with great flexibility about how we get there. This group of top leaders engaged with these questions and exercised them in the next stage of their joint learning effort. You can do that too.

Each of us can have a personal reciprocity advantage, if we can create it. There is a growing array of resources that can help you find your own reciprocity advantage and even places where you can go. Leaders today have new tools to help them create a reciprocity advantage.

New Tools and Resources

In Chapter 3, we introduced TechShop as an example of experimenting to learn. TechShop is a signal of a new kind of resource to help people make their own futures. TechShop is a business based on reciprocity. It is also a business that is designed to help people find their own personal reciprocity advantage. The sign outside TechShop's door says it all: Build Your Dreams Here. It could just as well say, "Create your own reciprocity advantage here." TechShop is just one of many resources that are becoming available with a wide range of new tools and practices.

TECHSHOP'S RECIPROCITY ADVANTAGE

What right-of-way does TechShop share with others? TechShop provides access to state-of-the-art maker tools, as well as links with other makers.

Who are TechShop partners? The original market was individual members who had personal projects or wanted to create prototypes to start new businesses. The new partners are large companies, many of whom (Autodesk, Ford, and DARPA) are using TechShop to spur creativity. Lowe's wants to support home improvement and do-it-yourself activities.

How did TechShop experiment to learn? The founder first ran a shop for the show *MythBusters*. Next, he operated a TechShop during the first Maker Faire in San Mateo, California. Then, TechShop opened up in nearby Menlo Park, putting out tools to share with other makers.

What assets did TechShop give away in order to learn? They set up the first shop and offered classes to find the recipe for a successful business.

How might TechShop scale? TechShops are being set up in other cities, and some companies, such as Ford, are cosponsoring similar efforts. As an independent business, this is scaling relatively slowly. But add 3D printers, the cloud, and a well-funded company like Lowe's or Home Depot, and TechShop could become what Geek Squad was for Best Buy.

What is TechShop's reciprocity advantage? TechShop enables a world of makers. It is the place to go to make or learn to make anything.

So What?

TechShop is a freestanding reciprocity business now. It is the state-of-the-art prototyping shop. And it's also a place where people can go to develop their own reciprocity advantages. Using the tools we provided for defining reciprocity businesses, how might people use TechShop—or other resources like it—to discover their own reciprocity advantages? The TechShop concept, as compelling as it is, has not yet scaled. Even if TechShop doesn't succeed commercially (but we think it will), it is a prototype for a wide range of new maker service businesses. TechShop is just one of what we expect will be a growing array of new resources to help individuals and organizations create their own reciprocity advantages.

Earlier we referenced William Gibson's now-famous insight: "The

EXAMPLES OF RECIPROCITY ADVANTAGES IN COMPANIES

Company	Reciprocity Advantage
TED	TEDx – the local version of TED staged anywhere
IBM	The Smarter Planet Initiative– big data know-how
Microsoft	Kinect platform for gestural interfaces
Global Food Safety Initiative	A strong, consistent approach to food safety with a low-cost solution that allows everyone to focus on higher-order benefits "Food safety is not a competitive advantage."
Google	Google Fiber, which allows Google to see the future sooner by removing the speed limitations and collecting usage data on all new platforms
Apple	The App Store, which has created a world of new businesses "There's an app for that."
TechShop	TechShops, where makers go to build their dreams

Source: Bob Johansen and Karl Ronn.

future is here already—it's just not evenly distributed." We believe that the future is reciprocity. In this book, we provide many early examples of companies who are already practicing reciprocity and are achieving a business advantage. Role models for reciprocity are all around us, if we learn to look carefully.

Here, in summary, are the basic criteria for deciding if a new venture is or is not a reciprocity advantage.

It will be a reciprocity advantage if it

- builds from an existing right-of-way that you already own;
- involves giving away some assets, while still retaining right-of-way;
- enhances your core business;
- requires partnering with others who have resources that the founding partner does not have—to do something that the founding partner could not do alone;

- makes money;
- is massively scalable.

It will *not* be a reciprocity advantage if it

- requires you to buy a right-of-way that you do not already own;
- cannibalizes the core business;
- hurts your core mission;
- is completely under your control.

What Can You Do Now?

Uncover your reciprocity right-of-way. Partner to do what you can't do alone. Experiment to learn. Amplify to create scale. Create your own reciprocity advantage. This model will work at the corporate level, but you can also use it on yourself to create your own personal reciprocity advantage.

The world of transactions—buying and selling stuff—will continue to exist, but it will become increasingly difficult to make money in this space alone. The core of any business will continue to be removing unnecessary costs and meeting the needs of existing customers. But companies will need new avenues of growth. Focusing on margin growth alone will not be sustainable. To drive growth, you will need to focus on increasing value for your customers, value that will grow overall market size. Master your transactional business, but grow it by creating your own reciprocity advantage.

We've showed you how to assess your current business and create a new reciprocity-advantage business. Your reciprocity advantage will create new opportunities for high-margin businesses that can complement your core business. In this book we have explored the future forces that will disrupt traditional businesses and create new growth opportunities, including analyses of how

- digital natives will disrupt rights-of-way;
- socialstructing will disrupt partnering;

- gameful engagement will disrupt experimenting to learn;
- cloud-served supercomputing will disrupt the practice of scaling.

You will have to engage with these disruptions to your current business and figure out how to create a reciprocity advantage.

Massively scalable reciprocity is the future. Many of the new giant businesses today are already practicing reciprocity advantage—even if they don't call it that. IBM, Apple, Amazon, Google, Airbnb, Facebook, and many others create new partnerships with thousands of people or companies in order to achieve extraordinary growth. We have showed you how you can do this yourself at low risk.

All businesses—and all individuals—have an opportunity to find a reciprocity advantage. Reciprocity and advantage, long thought of separately, will be increasingly synergistic.

NOTES

1. Nilofer Merchant, "When TED Lost Control of Its Crowd," *Harvard Business Review*, April 2013. http://hbr.org/2013/04/when-ted-lost-control-of-its-crowd/.

2. Chris Anderson, "TED Isn't a Recipe for 'Civilisational Disaster,'" the *Guardian*, January 8, 2014. http://www.theguardian.com/commentis free/2014/jan/08/ted-not-civilisational-disaster-but-wikipedia.

3. Michael E. Porter and Mark R. Kramer, "Creating Shared Value," *Harvard Business Review*, January 2011. http://hbr.org/2011/01/the-big-idea -creating-shared-value/ar/1.

4. *VUCA World* was coined, as best we can tell, at the U.S. Army War College in Carlisle, Pennsylvania. For more background, see Bob Johansen's *Leaders Make the Future: Ten New Leadership Skills for an Uncertain World* (San Francisco: Berrett-Koehler Publishers, 2012). In this book, Bob describes how, by looking ten years ahead, you can flip the threats of the VUCA World into opportunities. Part Two of this book describes those elements of the VUCA World that will shape scalable reciprocity.

5. There are links here to a larger mindset called Service-Dominant Logic (or S-D Logic, for short). "The foundational proposition of S-D logic is that organizations, markets, and society are fundamentally concerned with exchange of service. . . . That is, *service is exchanged for service*; all firms are service firms, all markets are centered on the exchange of service, and all economies and societies are service based." "What is SD Logic?" *Service-Dominant Logic.* Accessed February 28, 2014. http://sdlogic .net/.

6. 2012 IBM Annual Report. Accessed March 1, 2014. http://www.ibm
.com/annualreport/2012/bin/assets/2012_ibm_annual.pdf.

7. "IBM Watson's Next Venture: Fueling New Era of Cognitive Apps
Built in the Cloud by Developers," IBM News Room. Accessed November
14, 2013. http://www03.ibm.com/press/us/en/pressrelease/42451.wss.

8. Ibid.

9. 2012 IBM Annual Report, p. 9.

10. Ibid., p. 5.

11. "About Kinect for Windows," Microsoft Corporation.
Accessed March 1, 2014. http://www.microsoft.com/en-us/kinectfor
windows/news/about.aspx.

12. Meeting of the California Academy of Appellate Lawyers in
Carmel, California, on May 5, 2013. Quoted with permission from Judge
Alex Kozinski.

13. "About GFSI," Global Food Safety Initiative. Accessed March 1,
2014. http://www.mygfsi.com/about-gfsi.html.

14. Phil Crandall, Ellen J. Van Loo, Corliss A. O'Bryan, Andy
Mauromoustakos, Frank Yiannas, Natalie Dyenson, and Irina Berdnik,
"Companies' Opinions and Acceptance of Global Food Safety Initiative
Benchmarks after Implementation," *Journal of Food Protection* 75, no. 9
(2012): 1660–72. doi:10.4315/0362-028X.JFP-11-550.

15. This study was conducted by McCallum Layton in the fall of 2013
and first presented to the GFSI Board in Anaheim on February 28, 2014.
It was an online survey with 15,000 contacts in 21 countries covering
Western Europe, North America, Mexico, Australia, and New Zealand.

16. GE Global Innovation Barometer, Report, January 2013. http://
www.ge.com/sites/default/files/Innovation_Overview.pdf.

17. Brandon Bailey, "Ultrafast Google Fiber Seeks to Expand in
9 Metro Areas, Including San Jose," *San Jose Mercury News*, February
19, 2014. http://www.mercurynews.com/business/ci_25180109
/google-plans-big-expansion-fiber-internet-service-invites.

18. Johansen, *Leaders Make the Future.*

19. Mark Hatch, *The Maker Movement Manifesto: Rules for Innovation in
the New World of Crafters, Hackers, and Tinkerers* (New York: McGraw-Hill
Education, 2014), pp. 1–2.

20. We have heard this insight from Professor Reeves, but it is also
the motto of a successful business game design firm called Natron Baxter

in St. Louis. We've not been able to determine who said it first, but it is a wonderful insight.

21. Johansen, *Leaders Make the Future*, pp. 75–94.

22. Mister Jalopy, "Owner's Manifesto," Makezine.com. Accessed March 1, 2014. http://archive.makezine.com/04/ownyourown/.

23. Daniel Ben-Horin, "Innovation Obsession Disorder," *Stanford Innovation Review*, 10th Anniversary, April 11, 2012, p. 1.

24. On the occasion of the fifth anniversary of the App Store, Casey Newton did a good review of its history, "How Apple Changed the World Again: The App Store Turns Five," *The Verge*, July 10, 2013. http://www.theverge.com/2013/7/10/4507930/the-revolution-will-be-downloaded-the-app-store-turns-5.

25. Joshua Brustein, "Apple Users Spent $10 Billion on Apps in 2013," *Bloomberg Businessweek*, January 7, 2014. http://www.businessweek.com/articles/2014-01-07/apple-users-spent-10-billion-on-apps-in-2013#rshare=email_article.

26. "Job Creation," Apple. Accessed March 1, 2014. http://www.apple.com/about/job-creation/.

27. Micah Siegel and Fred Gibbons, "Amazon Enters the Cloud Computing Business," CasePublisher.com, May 20, 2008. http://www.stanford.edu/class/ee204/Publications/Amazon-EE353-2008-1.pdf.

28. Clay Shirky, *Here Comes Everybody: The Power of Organizing without Organizations* (New York: Penguin Press, 2008).

29. Kendall F. Haven, *Story Proof: The Science behind the Startling Power of Story* (Westport: Libraries Unlimited, 2007).

30. Quoted in *The Economist*, December 4, 2003, although he may have said it as early as August 31, 1993, in an interview on National Public Radio's *Fresh Air*.

31. Gregory C. Johnson, "The Entire IPCC Report in 19 Illustrated Haiku," *Sightline Daily*. Accessed March 1, 2014. http://daily.sightline.org/2013/12/16/the-entire-ipcc-report-in-19-illustrated-haiku/.

32. The term *VUCA* (Volatile, Uncertain, Complex, and Ambiguous) comes from the U.S. Army's graduate school in Pennsylvania but applies to business as well. Bob wrote an entire chapter called "The VUCA World: Both Danger and Opportunity" in his book *Get There Early: Sensing the Future to Compete in the Present*, pp. 24–44.

33. Milton Chen, Extreme Learners. Accessed March 1, 2014. http://extremelearners.iftf.org/.

34. Anya Kamenetz, *Generation Debt: Why Now Is a Terrible Time to Be Young* (New York: Riverhead Books/Penguin, 2006).

35. George Packer, "Change the World: Silicon Valley Transfers Its Slogans—and Money—to the Realm of Politics," the *New Yorker*, May 27, 2013.

36. Michael E. Conroy, *Branded!: How the "Certification Revolution" Is Transforming Global Corporations* (Gabriola Island, BC, Canada: New Society Publishers, 2007).

37. http://freespace.io.

38. Thomas L. Friedman, *The World Is Flat: A Brief History of the Twenty-first Century* (New York: Farrar, Straus and Giroux, 2005).

39. There will be fascinating opportunities for new research as this period unfolds. Evolutionary psychology has explored kinship-based cultures, which have strong roots in every major civilization, including China, India, and Greece. Adam Bellow's book *In Praise of Nepotism* explores the role of kinship ties in Western civilization and American democracy. Cloud-served supercomputing will create a new context for kinship.

40. Johansen, *Leaders Make the Future*, pp. 165–81.

41. Mark F. Schar, "Pivot Thinking and the Differential Sharing of Information within New Product Development Teams," Thesis, Stanford University, Dept. of Mechanical Engineering, 2011.

42. Theodore Levitt, "Marketing Myopia," *Harvard Business Review*, July/August 1960.

43. Scott D. Anthony, *The Innovator's Guide to Growth: Putting Disruptive Innovation to Work* (Boston: Harvard Business Press, 2008).

44. For more detail, go online to download the free tool kit for doing design thinking. http://www.ideo.com/work/toolkit-for-educators.

45. Howard Rheingold, *Smart Mobs: The Next Social Revolution* (Cambridge: Perseus, 2003).

46. William M. Klepper and Yoshi Tomozumi Nakamura, "Corporate Leadership and the Personal Leadership Credo," Fall 2011. http://www.gsb.columbia.edu/caseworks/node/380.

BIBLIOGRAPHY

"About GFSI." Global Food Safety Initiative. Accessed March 1, 2014. http://www.mygfsi.com/about-gfsi.html.

"About Kinect for Windows." Microsoft Corporation. Accessed March 1, 2014. http://www.microsoft.com/en-us/kinectforwindows/news/about.aspx.

Achor, Shawn. *The Happiness Advantage: The Seven Principles of Positive Psychology That Fuel Success and Performance at Work*. New York: Crown Business, 2010.

Anderson, Chris. *Free: How Today's Smartest Businesses Profit by Giving Something for Nothing*. New York: Hyperion, 2009.

Anderson, Chris. "TED Isn't a Recipe for 'Civilisational Disaster.'" the *Guardian*. January 8, 2014. Accessed January 10, 2014. www.theguardian.com/commentisfree/2014/jan/08 /ted-not-civilisational-disaster -but-wikipedia.

Anthony, Scott D. *The Little Black Book of Innovation: How It Works, How to Do It*. Boston: Harvard Business Review Press, 2012.

Anthony, Scott D., Mark W. Johnson, Joseph V. Sinfield, and Elizabeth J. Altman. *The Innovator's Guide to Growth: Putting Disruptive Innovation to Work*. Boston: Harvard Business Press, 2008.

Ariely, Dan. *The (Honest) Truth About Dishonesty: How We Lie to Everyone—Especially Ourselves*. New York: HarperCollins, 2012.

Bailey, Brandon. "Ultrafast Google Fiber Seeks to Expand in 9 Metro Areas, including San Jose." *San Jose Mercury News*. February 19, 2014. www.mercurynews.com/business/ci_25180109/google-plans-big -expansion-fiber-internet-service-invites.

Baxter, Natron. *Applied Gaming.* Accessed March 1, 2014. http://natron baxter.com/.

Bellow, Adam. *In Praise of Nepotism: A Natural History.* New York: Doubleday, 2003.

Botsman, Rachel, and Roo Rogers. *What's Mine Is Yours: The Rise of Collaborative Consumption.* New York: HarperBusiness, 2010.

Brown, Brené. *Daring Greatly: How the Courage to Be Vulnerable Transforms the Way We Live, Love, Parent, and Lead.* New York: Gotham Books, 2012.

Brown, Tim, and Barry Katz. *Change by Design: How Design Thinking Transforms Organizations and Inspires Innovation.* New York: HarperBusiness, 2009.

Brustein, Joshua. "Apple Users Spent $10 Billion on Apps in 2013." *Bloomberg Businessweek.* January 7, 2014. www.businessweek.com /articles/2014-01-07/apple-users-spent-10-billion-on-apps-in -2013#rshare=email_article.

Bstan-'dzin-rgya-mtsho. *Beyond Religion: Ethics for a Whole World.* New York: Houghton Mifflin Harcourt, 2011.

Cagan, Jonathan, and Craig M. Vogel. *Creating Breakthrough Products: Innovation from Product Planning to Program Approval.* Upper Saddle River: Prentice Hall PTR, 2002.

Castner, Brian. *The Long Walk: A Story of War and the Life That Follows.* New York: Anchor Books, 2012.

Chen, Milton. Extreme Learners. Accessed March 1, 2014. http://extreme learners.iftf.org/.

Christensen, Clayton M. *The Innovator's Dilemma: The Revolutionary Book That Will Change the Way You Do Business.* New York: HarperCollins, 2003.

Christensen, Clayton M., and Michael E. Raynor. *The Innovator's Solution: Creating and Sustaining Successful Growth.* Boston: Harvard Business School Press, 2003.

Christensen, Clayton M., James Allworth, and Karen Dillon. *How Will You Measure Your Life?* New York: HarperBusiness, 2012.

Cialdini, Robert B. *Influence: The Psychology of Persuasion.* New York: HarperBusiness, 2007.

Clark, David D. *Protecting the Internet as a Public Commons.* Cambridge: American Acad. of Arts and Sciences, 2011.

Coens, Tom, and Mary Jenkins. *Abolishing Performance Appraisals: Why*

They Backfire and What to Do Instead. San Francisco: Berrett-Koehler Publishers, 2002.

Conroy, Michael E. *Branded!: How the 'Certification Revolution' Is Transforming Global Corporations*. Gabriola Island, B.C., Canada: New Society Publishers, 2007.

Cox, Harvey. *The Future of Faith*. New York: HarperOne, 2009.

Crandall, Phil, Ellen J. Van Loo, Corliss A. O'Bryan, Andy Mauromoustakos, Frank Yiannas, Natalie Dyenson, and Irina Berdnik. "Companies' Opinions and Acceptance of Global Food Safety Initiative Benchmarks after Implementation." *Journal of Food Protection* 75, no. 9 (2012): 1660–72. doi:10.4315/0362-028X.JFP-11-550.

Dweck, Carol S. *Mindset: The New Psychology of Success*. New York: Ballantine Books, 2006.

Eichenwald, Kurt. *The Informant: A True Story*. New York: Broadway Books, 2001.

Eisenstein, Charles. *Sacred Economics: Money, Gift, and Society in the Age of Transition*. Berkeley: Evolver Editions, 2011.

Fallows, James M. *More Like Us*. Boston: Houghton Mifflin, 1990.

Fisher, Roger, William Ury, and Bruce Patton. *Getting to Yes: Negotiating Agreement without Giving In*. New York: Houghton Mifflin, 1991.

Fredrickson, Barbara L., *Love 2.0: How Our Supreme Emotion Affects Everything We Think, Do, Feel, and Become*. New York: Hudson Street Press, 2013.

Friedman, Edwin H. *A Failure of Nerve: Leadership in the Age of the Quick Fix*. Edited by Margaret M. Treadwell and Edward W. Beal. New York: Seabury Books, 2007.

Friedman, Edwin H. *Generation to Generation: Family Process in Church and Synagogue*. New York: Guilford Press, 2011.

Friedman, Thomas L. *The World Is Flat: A Brief History of the Twenty-first Century*. New York: Farrar, Straus and Giroux, 2005.

Fukuyama, Francis. *Trust: The Social Virtues and the Creation of Prosperity*. New York: Free Press, 1995.

Gansky, Lisa. *The Mesh: Why the Future of Business Is Sharing*. New York: Portfolio Penguin, 2010.

GE Global Innovation Barometer. Report. January 2013. http://www.ge .com/sites/default/files/Innovation_Overview.pdf.

Gorbis, Marina. *The Nature of the Future: Dispatches from the Socialstructed World*. New York: Free Press, 2013.

Grant, Adam M. *Give and Take: A Revolutionary Approach to Success*. New York: Viking, 2013.

Hagel, John, III, John Seely Brown, and Lang Davison. *The Power of Pull: How Small Moves, Smartly Made, Can Set Big Things in Motion*. New York: Basic Books, 2012.

Hatch, Mark. *The Maker Movement Manifesto: Rules for Innovation in the New World of Crafters, Hackers, and Tinkerers*. McGraw-Hill Education.

Haven, Kendall F. *Story Proof: The Science behind the Startling Power of Story*. Westport: Libraries Unlimited, 2007.

Hodge, Jack D. *The Power of Habit: Harnessing the Power to Establish Routines That Guarantee Success in Business and in Life*. Bloomington: 1stBooks, 2003.

Hsieh, Tony. *Delivering Happiness: A Path to Profits, Passion, and Purpose*. New York: Business Plus, 2010.

Hugos, Michael, and Derek Hulitzky. *Business in the Cloud: What Every Business Needs to Know about Cloud Computing*. New York: Wiley, 2011.

IBM 2012 Annual Report. Accessed March 1, 2014. http://www.ibm.com /annualreport/2012/bin/assets/2012_ibm_annual.pdf.

"IBM Watson's Next Venture: Fueling New Era of Cognitive Apps Built in the Cloud by Developers." IBM News Room. November 14, 2013. Accessed February 2, 2014. http://www-03.ibm.com/press/us/en /pressrelease/42451.wss.

Jalopy, Mister. "Owner's Manifesto." Makezine.com. Accessed March 1, 2014. http://archive.makezine.com/04/ownyourown/.

"Job Creation." Apple. Accessed March 1, 2014. http://www.apple.com /about/job-creation/.

Johansen, Bob. *Leaders Make the Future: Ten New Leadership Skills for an Uncertain World*. San Francisco: Berrett-Koehler Publishers, 2012.

Johnson, Gregory C. "The Entire IPCC Report in 19 Illustrated Haiku." *Sightline Daily*. Accessed March 1, 2014. http://daily.sightline.org/2013 /12/16/the-entire-ipcc-report-in-19-illustrated-haiku/.

Johnson, Mark W. *Seizing the White Space: Business Model Innovation for Growth and Renewal*. Boston: Harvard Business Press, 2010.

Johnson, Steven. *Where Good Ideas Come From: The Natural History of Innovation*. New York: Riverhead Books, 2010.

Kamenetz, Anya. *Generation Debt: Why Now Is a Terrible Time to Be Young*. New York: Penguin, 2006.

Kiefer, Charles F., and Malcolm Constable. *The Art of Insight: How to Have More Aha! Moments.* San Francisco: Berrett-Koehler Publishers, 2013.

Klepper, William M., and Yoshi Tomozumi Nakamura. "Corporate Leadership and the Personal Leadership Credo." Corporate Leadership and the Personal Leadership Credo. Fall 2011. http://www8.gsb.columbia.edu/caseworks/node/380.

Lafley, A. G., and Roger L. Martin. *Playing to Win: How Strategy Really Works.* Boston: Harvard Business Review Press, 2013.

Lehrer, Jonah. *Imagine: How Creativity Works.* New York: Houghton Mifflin Harcourt, 2012.

Levitt, Theodore. "Marketing Myopia." *Harvard Business Review,* July/August 1960.

Lynch, Caitrin. *Retirement on the Line: Age, Work, and Value in an American Factory.* Ithaca: Cornell University Press, 2012.

Macy, Joanna, and Chris Johnstone. *Active Hope: How to Face the Mess We're in without Going Crazy.* Novato: New World Library, 2012.

Markel, Howard. *An Anatomy of Addiction: Sigmund Freud, William Halsted, and the Miracle Drug Cocaine.* New York: Pantheon Books, 2011.

McGonigal, Jane. *Reality Is Broken: Why Games Make Us Better and How They Can Change the World.* New York: Penguin Press, 2011.

McGrath, Rita Gunther, and Ian C. MacMillan. *Discovery-Driven Growth: A Breakthrough Process to Reduce Risk and Seize Opportunity.* Boston: Harvard Business Press, 2009.

Merchant, Nilofer. "When TED Lost Control of Its Crowd." *Harvard Business Review,* April 2013. http://hbr.org/2013/04/when-ted-lost-control-of-its-crowd/.

Naím, Moisés. *The End of Power: From Boardrooms to Battlefields and Churches to States, Why Being in Charge Isn't What It Used to Be.* New York: Basic Books, 2013.

Newton, Casey. "How Apple Changed the World Again: The App Store Turns Five." *The Verge.* July 10, 2013. www.theverge.com/2013/7/10/4507930/the-revolution-will-be-downloaded-the-app-store-turns-5.

Packer, George. "Change the World: Silicon Valley Transfers Its Slogans—and Money—to the Realm of Politics." the *New Yorker,* May 27, 2013, 51.

Pine, B. Joseph, II, and James H. Gilmore. *The Experience Economy.* Boston: Harvard Business Review Press, 2011.

Porter, Michael E., and Mark R. Kramer. "Creating Shared Value." *Harvard Business Review.* January 2011. http://hbr.org/2011/01/the-big -idea-creating-shared-value/ar/1.

Pretzer, William S. *Working at Inventing: Thomas A. Edison and the Menlo Park Experience.* Baltimore: Johns Hopkins University Press, 2001.

Prothero, Stephen R. *God Is Not One: The Eight Rival Religions That Run the World—and Why Their Differences Matter.* New York: HarperCollins, 2010.

Rheingold, Howard. *Smart Mobs: The Next Social Revolution.* Cambridge: Perseus, 2003.

Schar, Mark F. "Pivot Thinking and the Differential Sharing of Information within New Product Development Teams." Thesis, Stanford University, Dept. of Mechanical Engineering, 2011.

Schwartz, Barry, and Kenneth Sharpe. *Practical Wisdom: The Right Way to Do the Right Thing.* New York: Riverhead Books, 2010.

"Service-Dominant Logic." Service-Dominant Logic. Accessed February 28, 2014. http://sdlogic.net/.

Shirky, Clay. *Cognitive Surplus: Creativity and Generosity in a Connected Age.* New York: Penguin Press, 2010.

Shirky, Clay. *Here Comes Everybody: The Power of Organizing without Organizations.* New York: Penguin Press, 2008.

Sibbet, David. *Visual Leaders: New Tools for Visioning, Management, and Organization Change.* Hoboken: John Wiley & Sons, 2013.

Sibbet, David. *Visual Teams: Graphic Tools for Commitment, Innovation, and High Performance.* Hoboken: John Wiley & Sons, 2011.

Siegel, Micah, and Fred Gibbons. "Amazon Enters the Cloud Computing Business." CasePublisher.com. May 20, 2008. http://www.stanford.edu /class/ee204/Publications/Amazon-EE353-2008-1.pdf.

Stone, Linda. "Continuous Partial Attention." Accessed March 1, 2014. http://lindastone.net/qa/continuous-partial-attention/.

"Study Elaborates on GFSI Results." *Cleaning and Maintenance Management Online.* February 27, 2014. http://www.cmmonline.com /articles/233045-study-elaborates-on-gfsi-results.

Suarez, Daniel. *Daemon.* New York: Signet, 2010.

Taber, George M. *Judgment of Paris: California vs. France and the Historic 1976 Paris Tasting That Revolutionized Wine.* New York: Scribner, 2006.

Wagner, Tony. *Creating Innovators: The Making of Young People Who Will Change the World.* New York: Scribner, 2012.

Wheatley, Margaret J. *So Far from Home—Lost and Found in Our Brave New World.* 1st ed. San Francisco: Berrett-Koehler, 2012.

Wright, Robert. *Nonzero: The Logic of Human Destiny.* New York: Vintage Books, 2000.

ACKNOWLEDGMENTS

When coauthoring a book works, it is a magical experience. One author goes as far as he can and ends exhausted, sending it off to the other coauthor. When the manuscript comes back to the first author, it has improved in ways that would not have been possible if each author were working alone. This has been that kind of writing experience for us both. We've written a book that neither of us could have done alone. We now realize we were both in search of our own reciprocity advantage. We both gave all we had to the book, but we got back so much more from each other.

Our thanks to others is deeply felt. We begin with our editor Steve Piersanti, the founder of the remarkable publisher called Berrett-Koehler. Steve is not only a great editor, he is the best editor that either of us could imagine. He inspired us, he pushed us, and he stretched us. He was truly a partner in our thinking about reciprocity, and it was Steve who came up with the juxtaposition of reciprocity and advantage that is core to the book. We have had remarkable support from BK and all its staff. Dave Peattie and Tanya Grove of BookMatters worked diligently with us to provide excellent copyediting, interior book design, and production assistance.

Two outside reviewers were particularly important in shaping this book—we are so grateful to Danielle Goodman and Valerie Andrews. Archie Ferguson worked so patiently with us to create the cover design in a way that visualized the logic of the book and added a design flare. We could not have done without him.

Our research assistant for this book was Alessandro Voto, and he is so much more than an assistant. Alex taught us economics and helped us into the space of reciprocity-based economics. He was diligent and demanding in his own amazingly productive way, always adding value to every task. He also provided us with cross-generational mentoring when we needed it, which was often.

Laurel Funkhouser manages Bob's calendar with great personal care and was instrumental in keeping this project on time and on task. Thanks, Laurel!

Our colleagues at Institute for the Future have been invaluable at each stage. Certainly, this is a book that draws heavily upon the continuous stream of foresight coming from IFTF. Bob works full-time with IFTF, and Karl has been a client for many years. In particular, we want to thank Marina Gorbis, IFTF's executive director, and her remarkable research on "socialstructing," which we draw upon heavily in Chapter 10. It is so difficult to mention everyone who has contributed to the book in specific ways from Institute for the Future, but here is our best attempt. Kathi Vian, leader of the IFTF annual Ten-Year Forecast, has been very generous and supportive, and her content infuses this book. Devin Fidler worked with us on early drafts and was very helpful roughing out some of the core concepts. We have also gained so much from the IFTF community, especially Jason Tester, Miriam Lueck Avery, Sean Ness, Jake Dunagan, Jean Hagan, Dylan Hendricks, Lyn Jeffery, Brad Kreit, Rachel Hatch, Anthony Townsend, Mike Liebhold, David Pescovitz, and Rachel Maguire. IFTF is truly a community of researchers, and the community has added so much to our thinking. The current IFTF core team includes Jamais Cascio, Adam Elmaghraby, Alex Goldman, Andy Lam, Ben Hamamoto, Bettina Warburg-Johnson, David Harris, Dawn Alva, Eri Gentry, Ken Harootunian, Kim Lawrence, Marty Low, Maureen Kirchner, Neela Lazkani, Nic Weidinger, Rebecca Chesney, Robin Bogott, Rod Falcon, Sara Skvirsky, Sarah Smith, and Tessa Finlev. Thanks also to the current IFTF board of directors, including Ellen Marram, Aron Cramer, Debra Engel, Karen Edwards, and Michael Kleeman.

Scott Anthony and the team at Innosight have been in the trenches, turning Clay Christensen's insights into action. Karl has been fortunate to be on that same journey, often together with them, for the last decade.

Tim Brown, Dennis Boyle, the Kelley brothers, and the whole group at IDEO has been inspirational and personally supportive. Thanks for often letting Karl be an honorary member of the IDEO team.

And there is no better extended family than current and former Procter & Gamble leaders. Thanks to you all. Nabil Sakaab and Gordon Brunner are masters of changing the rules of the game. Tom Finn's experience in partnering is essential to those insights in this book. Scott Cook, one of those ex-P&Gers, is one of Silicon Valley's sage voices for innovation and one of the genuinely good guys.

Taylor McConnell helped Bob think through some of the basic concepts of reciprocity. Taylor was on Bob's doctoral committee at Northwestern and continues to provide wonderful mentoring, insight, and friendship.

We have learned so much over the last few years of developing and testing the concept of reciprocity advantage. While we cannot list everyone here, we want to make it clear that the workshops we have done with a wide range of organizations has been so helpful to us in clarifying our thinking. This book began in the talks that we have given over the last few years for organizations like Procter & Gamble, Kellogg's, Disney, Anheuser-Busch InBev, Intel, Walmart, Syngenta, Johnson & Johnson, UPS, McKinsey, General Mills, Tesco, China Fortune Land Development, First Pacific, Cisco, and McDonald's.

Jim Spohrer from IBM Almaden Research was particularly helpful in clarifying the emerging concept of service science and understanding IBM's Smarter Planet initiative.

The thinking of Judge Alex Kozinski gave us great insight into the delicacies of intellectual property in the world of reciprocity advantage.

Lisa Mumbach and Anthony Weeks helped us imagine and visualize the key concepts of reciprocity. Both Lisa and Anthony worked with us from the start, and we are so grateful to them for helping us visualize even before we could find the right words. "Visual storytelling," Anthony calls it, and we are avid students.

Rachael Shander from Williams-Sonoma is a remarkable leader who worked with us on the possibilities for applying reciprocity advantage to personal leadership learning.

Stephen Bennett from United Cerebral Palsy and Rich Donovan from Return on Disability were both very helpful to us in understanding how business engagement with people with disabilities can be a very important form of reciprocity advantage.

Our wives, Robin and Elizabeth, have been partners in each stage of our thinking. You are inspiring and have contributed so much to the book and to our mental health as we have completed the book. We are both truly blessed.

Finally, Bob did much of his writing at Kaffeehaus in San Mateo. A good coffee house does so much to contribute to good writing. Thanks Val! Karl survived on Delta Airlines coffee, but being locked in a seat for endless hours does help turn insight into action when it comes to writing.

INDEX

Bob Johansen (left) and **Karl Ronn** (right) bring together two different rights-of-way, based on their years of experience in extremely different worlds before they came together to write this book.

Bob has been helping organizations around the world prepare for and shape the future for more than thirty years. This is Bob's tenth book. He is a frequent keynote speaker for large groups and leads a wide range of workshops with rising-star leaders.

Prior to starting his own innovation firm, Karl was Vice President of Research and Development and General Manager of New Business for The Procter & Gamble Company. Swiffer, Febreze, and Mr. Clean Magic Eraser are billion-dollar businesses he helped to create and grow.

Bob and Karl have partnered in this book to do something that neither could have done alone. They mix the futures view—looking ten years out and beyond—with the voice of practical but disruptive innovation.

We had the idea for this book as we flew home together from the Philippines after working together with a large Asian company trying to remake its future. We imagined a new partnership that would allow us to explore the intersection of foresight and business innovation. This book is the first fruit of our working relationship.

To write this book, we experimented to learn over the last four years in a wide variety of projects, workshops, and talks. As a distinguished fellow at IFTF, Bob draws on his training in the social sciences and his extensive experience at the edges of multiple disciplines as he interacts with top leaders of business, government, and nonprofit organizations to encourage thoughtful consideration of the long-term future. His most recent book, the second edition of *Leaders Make the Future: Ten New Leadership Skills for an Uncertain Age*, has contributions from the Center for Creative Leadership. Connect Consulting Group named this book on change management and leadership as the best business book of 2012. Bob has done workshops based on his books at a wide range of corporations, including P&G, Kellogg's, Disney, Intel, Walmart, Syngenta, Johnson & Johnson, UPS, McKinsey, General Mills, and McDonald's. Major universities, nonprofits, and churches also use his books.

Karl is now Managing Director of Innovation Portfolio Partners, a Silicon Valley–based firm that helps CEOs and the top management of Fortune 500 companies find and develop new products and services. He also cofounded VC-backed Butterfly Health which created Butterfly body liners, and he is developing a software company that builds diagnostic competency for physicians using virtual human simulations of top medical school cases.

The Reciprocity Advantage is Bob and Karl's effort to scale their thinking and experience about both the very human instinct toward reciprocity and the business requirement to seek advantage. Over the last years of testing, they have learned and now documented in this book that reciprocity advantage is desirable, viable, and sustainable. Now is the time to scale it.

Born in Geneva, Illinois, Bob holds a BS from the University of Illinois, where he attended on a basketball scholarship and channeled his unrealistic desire to be a professional athlete. He received a PhD from Northwestern University, where he was introduced to the Internet (then called the ARPANet) as it was just coming to life.

In addition, Bob has a divinity school degree from Crozer Theological Seminary, where he began his lifelong interest in world religions, ethics, and things spiritual. Bob was the president of the Institute for the Future for eight years and founded its program of research on emerging technology horizons.

Born in Cleveland, Ohio, Karl was graduated from the University of Toledo with a degree in chemical engineering. In his thirty years with P&G, Karl was responsible for the global R&D for pharmaceuticals and over-the-counter health care products, including Actonel, Vicks, Prilosec, and in-home diagnostic tests. Prior to health care, he was responsible for household cleaning products and Gillette's Duracell batteries. He has also managed beauty care businesses and started diaper and Maxipad businesses across Latin America. Corporately, he helped develop the company's capability to create disruptive innovations.

Karl is on the advisory boards of the Johns Hopkins Bloomberg School of Public Health and University of Toledo. He is a former board member of the Cincinnati Symphony Orchestra, which gave him a chance to channel his unrealistic desire to be a musician. He is a member of TED Conference and has been a speaker at the Mayo Clinic, Consumer Medical Conference, American Medical Association, and other innovation forums.

Bob is married to Robin B. Johansen, an attorney practicing constitutional law. They have two children and three grandchildren.

Karl is married to Elizabeth Hodge Ronn, a former P&G Marketing Vice President. They have two children who were born while they were living in Venezuela.

Berrett–Koehler
Publishers

Berrett-Koehler is an independent publisher dedicated to an ambitious mission: *Creating a World That Works for All*.

We believe that to truly create a better world, action is needed at all levels—individual, organizational, and societal. At the individual level, our publications help people align their lives with their values and with their aspirations for a better world. At the organizational level, our publications promote progressive leadership and management practices, socially responsible approaches to business, and humane and effective organizations. At the societal level, our publications advance social and economic justice, shared prosperity, sustainability, and new solutions to national and global issues.

A major theme of our publications is "Opening Up New Space." Berrett-Koehler titles challenge conventional thinking, introduce new ideas, and foster positive change. Their common quest is changing the underlying beliefs, mindsets, institutions, and structures that keep generating the same cycles of problems, no matter who our leaders are or what improvement programs we adopt.

We strive to practice what we preach—to operate our publishing company in line with the ideas in our books. At the core of our approach is stewardship, which we define as a deep sense of responsibility to administer the company for the benefit of all of our "stakeholder" groups: authors, customers, employees, investors, service providers, and the communities and environment around us.

We are grateful to the thousands of readers, authors, and other friends of the company who consider themselves to be part of the "BK Community." We hope that you, too, will join us in our mission.

A BK Business Book

This book is part of our BK Business series. BK Business titles pioneer new and progressive leadership and management practices in all types of public, private, and nonprofit organizations. They promote socially responsible approaches to business, innovative organizational change methods, and more humane and effective organizations.

Berrett–Koehler
Publishers

A community dedicated to creating
a world that works for all

Dear Reader,

Thank you for picking up this book and joining our worldwide community of Berrett-Koehler readers. We share ideas that bring positive change into people's lives, organizations, and society.

To welcome you, we'd like to offer you a free e-book. You can pick from among twelve of our bestselling books by entering the promotional code **BKP92E** here: http://www.bkconnection.com/welcome.

When you claim your free e-book, we'll also send you a copy of our e-newsletter, the *BK Communiqué*. Although you're free to unsubscribe, there are many benefits to sticking around. In every issue of our newsletter you'll find

- A free e-book
- Tips from famous authors
- Discounts on spotlight titles
- Hilarious insider publishing news
- A chance to win a prize for answering a riddle

Best of all, our readers tell us, "Your newsletter is the only one I actually read." So claim your gift today, and please stay in touch!

Sincerely,

Charlotte Ashlock
Steward of the BK Website

Questions? Comments? Contact me at bkcommunity@bkpub.com.

Certified

Corporation
bcorporation.net